E C C O
Travels

Smara: The Forbidden City by Michel Vieuchange
Italian Hours by Henry James
Amyntas by André Gide
Pictures from Italy by Charles Dickens
The Journey's Echo by Freya Stark
Augustus Hare in Italy
The Spanish Temper by V. S. Pritchett
Italian Backgrounds by Edith Wharton

Forthcoming:
Along the Road by Aldous Huxley
Remote People by Evelyn Waugh
A Land by Jacquetta Hawkes

ITALIAN BACKGROUNDS

ITALIAN BACKGROUNDS

BY

EDITH WHARTON

ILLUSTRATED BY E. C. PEIXOTTO

THE ECCO PRESS
New York

First published in 1989 by The Ecco Press
26 West 17th Street, New York, NY 10011
Published simultaneously in Canada by
Penguin Books Ltd., Ontario
Printed in the United States of America
Cover by Beth Tondreau Design

Library of Congress Cataloging-in-Publication Data

Wharton, Edith, 1862–1937.
Italian backgrounds / by Edith Wharton;
illustrated by E. C. Peixotto.
p.   cm. — (Ecco travels)
Reprint. Originally published: New York: Scribner, 1905.
1. Italy—Description and travel—1901–1944.
2. Wharton, Edith, 1862–1937—Journeys—Italy.
3. Authors, American—20th century—Journeys.
I. Title   II. Series.
DG428.W44   1989   914.5′049—dc 19   88-30409

ISBN 0-88001-185-8

TABLE OF CONTENTS

LIST OF ILLUSTRATIONS

AN ALPINE POSTING-INN

AN ALPINE POSTING-INN

TO the mind curious in contrasts—surely one of the chief pleasures of travel—there can be no better preparation for a descent into Italy than a sojourn among the upper Swiss valleys. To pass from the region of the obviously picturesque —the country contrived, it would seem, for the delectation of the *cœur à poésie facile*—to that sophisticated landscape where the face of nature seems moulded by the passions and imaginings of man, is one of the most suggestive transitions in the rapidly diminishing range of such experiences.

Nowhere is this contrast more acutely felt than in one of the upper Grisons villages. The anecdotic Switzerland of the lakes is too remote from Italy, geographically and morally, to evoke a comparison. The toy chalet, with its air of self-conscious neatness, making one feel that if one lifted the roof it would disclose a row of tapes and scissors, or the shining cylinders of a musical box, suggests cabinet-work rather than architecture; the swept and garnished streets, the precise gardens, the subjugated vines, present the image of an old maid's paradise that would be thrown into hopeless disarray by the introduction of anything so irregular as a work of art. In the Grisons, however, where only a bald grey pass divides one from Italy, its influence is felt, in a negative sense, in the very untidiness of the streets, the rank growth of weeds along the base of rough glaring walls, the drone of flies about candidly-exposed manure-heaps. More agreeably, the same influence shows itself in the rude old centaur-like houses, with their wrought-iron window-grilles and stone escutcheons surmounting the odorous darkness of a stable. These are the houses of people conscious of Italy, who have transplanted to their bleak heights, either from poverty of invention, or an impulse as sentimental as our modern habit of "collecting," the thick walls, the small windows, the jutting eaves of dwellings designed under a sultry sky. So vivid is the reminiscence that one almost expects to see a cypress leaning against the bruised-peach-coloured walls of the village *douane;* but it is just here that the contrast accentuates itself. The cypress, with all it stands for, is missing.

It is not easy, in the height of the Swiss season, to light on a nook neglected by the tourist; but at Splügen he still sweeps by in a cloud of diligence dust, or pauses only to gulp a flask of Paradiso and a rosy trout from the Suretta lakes. One's enjoyment of the place is thus enhanced by the pleasing spectacle of the misguided hundreds who pass it by, and from the vantage of the solitary meadows above the village one may watch the throngs descending on Thusis or Chiavenna with something of the satisfaction that mediæval schoolmen believed to be the portion of angels looking down upon the damned. Splügen abounds in such points of observation. On all sides one may climb from the alder-fringed shores of the Rhine, through larch-thickets tremulous with the leap of water, to grassy levels far above, whence the valley is seen lengthening southward to a great concourse of peaks. In the morning these upper meadows are hot and bright, and one is glad of the red-aisled pines and the onyx-coloured torrents cooling the dusk; but toward sunset, when the shadows make the slopes of turf look like an expanse of tumbled velvet, it is pleasant to pace the open ledges, watching the sun recede from the valley, where mowers are still sweeping the grass into long curved lines like ridges of the sea, while the pine-woods on the eastern slopes grow black and the upper snows fade to the colour of cold ashes.

The landscape is simple, spacious and serene. The fields suggest the tranquil rumination of generations of cattle, the woods offer cool security to sylvan life, the mountains present blunt weather-beaten surfaces rather than the subtle contours, wrinkled as by meditation, of the Italian Alps. One feels that it is a scene in which *nothing has ever happened;* the haunting adjective is that which Whitman applies to the American landscape—" the large *unconscious* scenery of my native land."

Switzerland is like a dinner served in the old-fashioned way, with all the dishes put on the table at once: every valley has its flowery mead, its "horrid" gorge, its chamois-haunted peaks, its wood and water-fall. In Italy, the effects are brought on in courses, and memory is thus able to differentiate the landscapes, even without the help of that touch of human individuality to which, after all, the best

Italian scenery is but a setting. At Splügen, as in most Swiss landscapes, the human interest—the evidences of man's presence—are an interruption rather than a climax. The village of Splügen, huddled on a ledge above the Rhine, sheepishly turns the backs of its houses on the view, as though conscious of making a poor show compared to the tremendous performance of nature. Between these houses, set at unconsidered angles, like boxes hastily piled on a shelf, cobble-stone streets ramble up the hill; but after a few yards they lapse into mountain paths, and the pastures stoop unabashed to the back doors of the village. Agriculture seems, in fact, the little town's excuse for being. The whole of Splügen, in midsummer, is as one arm at the end of a scythe. All day long the lines of stooping figures—men, women and children, grandfathers and industrious babes—spread themselves over the hill-sides in an ever-widening radius, interminably cutting, raking and stacking the grass. The lower slopes are first laid bare; then, to the sheer upper zone of pines, the long grass, thick with larkspur, mountain pink and orchis, gradually recedes before the rising tide of mowers. Even in the graveyard of the high-perched

church, the scythes swing between mounds over-
grown with campanulas and martagon lilies; so that
one may fancy the dust of generations of thrifty
villagers enriching the harvests of posterity.

This, indeed, is the only destiny one can imagine
for them. The past of such a place must have been
as bucolic as its present: the mediæval keep, crumbling on its wooded spur above the Rhine, was surely
perched there that the lords of the valley might have
an eye to the grazing cattle and command the ma-
nœuvres of the mowers. The noble Georgiis who
lived in the escutcheoned houses of Splügen, and
now lie under such a wealth of quarterings in the
church and graveyard, must have been experts in
fertilizers and stock-raising; nor can one figure, even
for the seventeenth-century mercenary of the name,
whose epitaph declares him to have been "captain
of his Spanish Majesty's cohorts," emotions more
poignant, when he came home from the wars, than
that evoked by the tinkle of cow-bells in the pasture,
and the vision of a table groaning with smoked beef
and cyclopean cheeses.

So completely are the peasants in the fields a part
of the soil they cultivate, that during the day one

may be said to have the whole of Splügen to one's self, from the topmost peaks to the deserted high-road. In the evening the scene changes; and the transformation is not unintentionally described in theatrical terms, since the square which, after sunset, becomes the centre of life in Splügen, has an absurd resemblance to a stage-setting. One side of this square is bounded by the long weather-beaten front of the posting-inn—but the inn deserves a parenthe-sis. Built long ago, and then abandoned, so the vil-lage tradition runs, by a " great Italian family," its exterior shows the thick walls, projecting eaves and oval attic openings of an old Tuscan house; while within, a monastic ramification of stone-vaulted cor-ridors leads to rooms ceiled and panelled with six-teenth-century woodwork. The stone terrace before this impressive dwelling forms the proscenium where, after dinner, the spectators assemble. To the right of the square stands the pale pink " Post and Tele-graph Bureau." Beyond, closing in the right wing at a stage-angle, is a mysterious yellowish house with an arched entrance. Facing these, on the left, are the *dépendance* of the inn and the custom-house; in the left background, the village street is seen winding down, between houses that look like "studies" in old-fashioned drawing-books (with the cracks in the plaster done in very black lead), to the bridge across the Rhine and the first loops of the post-road over the Splügen pass. Opposite the inn is the obligatory village fountain, the rallying-point of the chorus; beneath a stone parapet flows the torrent which acts as an invisible orchestra; and beyond the parapet, snow peaks fill the background of the stage.

Dinner over, the eager spectators, hastening to the terrace (with a glimpse, as they pass the vaulted kitchen, of the Italian *chef* oiling his bicycle amid the débris of an admirable meal), find active preparations afoot for the event of the evening—the arrival of the diligences. Already the orchestra is tuning its instruments, and the chorus, recruited from the hay-fields, are gathering in the wings. A dozen of them straggle in and squat on the jutting stone basement of the post-office; others hang picturesquely about the fountain, or hover up the steep street, awaiting the prompter's call. Presently some of the subordinate characters stroll across the stage: the owner of the saw-mill on the Rhine, a tall man in homespun, deferentially saluted by the chorus; two personages in black coats, with walking-sticks, who always appear together, and have the air of being joint syndics of the village; a gentleman of leisure, in a white cap with a visor, smoking a long Italian cigar and attended by an inquisitive Pomeranian dog; a citizen in white socks and carpet slippers, giving his arm to his wife, and preceded by a Bewickian little boy with a green butterfly-box over his shoulder; the gold-braided custom-house officer hurrying up rather late for his cue; two or three local ladies in sunburnt millinery and spectacles, who drop in to see the post-mistress; and a showy young man, with the look of having seen life at Chur or Bellinzona, who emerges from the post-office conspicuously reading a letter, to the undisguised interest of the chorus, the ladies and the Pomeranian. As these figures pass and repass in a kind of social silence, they suggest the leisurely opening of some play composed before the unities were abolished, and peopled by types with generic names—the Innkeeper, the Postmistress, the Syndic —some comedy of Goldoni's, perhaps, but void even of Goldoni's simple malice.

Meanwhile the porter has lit the oil-lanterns hanging by a chain over the door of the inn; a celestial

hand has performed a similar office for the evening
star above the peaks; and through the hush that has
settled on the square comes a distant sound of bells.
. . . Instantly the action begins; the innkeeper ap-
pears, supported by the porter and the waiter; a wave
of acclamation runs through the chorus; the Pomeranian trots down the road; and presently the fagged
leaders of the Thusis diligence turn their heads round
the corner of the square. The preposterous yellow
coach—a landau attached to a glass "clarence"—
crosses the cobble-paved stage, swinging round with
a grand curve to the inn door; vague figures, detach-
ing themselves from the chorus, flit about the horses
or help the guard to lift the luggage down; the two
syndics, critically aloof, lean on their sticks to watch
the scene; the Pomeranian bustles between the tired
horses' legs; and the diligence doors let out a menagerie of the strange folk whom one sees only on one's
travels. Here they come, familiar as the figures in
a Noah's ark: Germans first—the little triple-chinned
man with a dachshund, out of "Fliegende Blätter,"
the slippered Hercules with a face like that at the end
of a meerschaum pipe, and their sentimental females;
shrill and vivid Italians, a pleasant pig-faced priest,

Americans going "right through," with their city and state writ large upon their luggage; English girls like navvies, and Frenchmen like girls; the arched doorway absorbs them, and another jingle of bells, and a flash of lamps on the bridge, proclaim that the Chiavenna diligence is coming.

The same ceremony repeats itself; and another detachment of the travelling menagerie descends. This time there is a family of rodents, who look as though they ought to be enclosed in wire netting and judiciously nourished on lettuce; there is a small fierce man in knickerbockers and a sash, conducting a large submissive wife and two hypocritical little boys who might have stepped out of "The Mirror of the Mind"; there is an unfortunate lady in spectacles, who looks like one of the Creator's rejected experiments, and carries a grey linen bag embroidered with forget-me-nots; there is the inevitable youth with an alpenstock, who sends home a bunch of edelweiss to his awe-struck family. . . . These, too, disappear; the horses are led away; the chorus disperses, the lights go out, the performance is over. Only one spectator lingers, a thoughtful man in a snuff-coloured overcoat, who gives the measure of the social

resources of Splügen by the deliberate way in which,
evening after evening, he walks around the empty
diligences, looks into their windows, examines the
wheels and poles, and then mournfully vanishes into
darkness.

At last the two diligences have the silent square to
themselves. There they stand, side by side in dusty
slumber, till the morning cow-bells wake them to departure. One goes back to Thusis; to the region of
good hotels, pure air and scenic platitudes. It may
go empty for all we care. But the other . . . the
other wakes from its Alpine sleep to climb the cold
pass at sunrise and descend by hot windings into the
land where the church steeples turn into *campanili,*
where the vine, breaking from perpendicular bond-
age, flings a liberated embrace about the mulberries,
and far off, beyond the plain, the mirage of domes
and spires, of painted walls and sculptured altars,
beckons across the dustiest tracts of memory. In
that diligence our seats are taken.

A MIDSUMMER WEEK'S DREAM

A MIDSUMMER WEEK'S DREAM

AUGUST IN ITALY

. . . . Un paysage choisi
Que vont charmant masques et bergamasques.

I

FOR ten days we had not known what ailed us.
We had fled from the August heat and
crowd of the Vorderrheinthal to the posting-
inn below the Splügen pass; and here fortune had
given us all the midsummer tourist can hope for—
solitude, cool air and fine scenery. A dozen times a
day we counted our mercies, but still privately felt
them to be insufficient. As we walked through the
larch-groves beside the Rhine, or climbed the grassy
heights above the valley, we were oppressed by the
didactic quality of our surroundings—by the aggres-
sive salubrity and repose of this *bergerie de Florian.*
We seemed to be living in the landscape of a sanato-
rium prospectus. It was all pleasant enough, ac-

cording to Schopenhauer's definition of pleasure. We had none of the things we did not want; but then we did not particularly want any of the things we had. We had fancied we did till we got them; and as we had to own that they did their part in fulfilling our anticipations, we were driven to conclude that the fault was in ourselves. Then suddenly we found out what was wrong. Splügen was charming, but it was too near Italy.

One can forgive a place three thousand miles from Italy for not being Italian; but that a village on the very border should remain stolidly, immovably Swiss was a constant source of exasperation. Even the landscape had neglected its opportunities. A few miles off it became the accomplice of man's most exquisite imaginings; but here we could see in it only endless material for Swiss clocks and fodder.

The trouble began with our watching the diligences. Every evening we saw one toiling up the pass from Chiavenna, with dusty horses and perspiring passengers. How we pitied those passengers! We walked among them puffed up with all the good air in our lungs. We felt fresh and cool and enviable, and moralized on the plaintive lot of those whose scant holidays compelled them to visit Italy in August. But already the poison was at work. We pictured what our less fortunate brothers had seen till we began to wonder if, after all, they were less fortunate. At least they had *been there;* and what drawbacks could qualify that fact? Was it better to be cool and look at a water-fall, or to be hot and look at Saint Mark's? Was it better to walk on gentians or on mosaic, to smell fir-needles or incense? Was it, in short, ever well to be elsewhere when one might be in Italy?

We tried to quell the rising madness by interrogating the travellers. Was it very hot on the lakes and in Milan? "Terribly!" they answered, and mopped their brows. "Unimaginative idiots!" we grumbled, and forbore to question the next batch. Of course it was hot there—but what of that? Think of the compensations! To take it on the lowest plane, think of the empty hotels and railway carriages, the absence of tourists and Baedekers! Even the Italians were away, among the Apennines and in the Engadine; we should have the best part of the country to ourselves. Gradually we began to picture our sensations should we take seats in the diligence on its return journey. From that moment we were lost. We did not say much to each other, but one morning at sunrise we found a travelling-carriage at the door. No one seemed to know who had ordered it, but we noticed that our luggage was being strapped on behind. We took our seats and the driver turned his horses toward the Splügen pass. It was not the way to Switzerland.

We mounted to ice and snow. The savage landscape led us to the top of the pass and dogged us down to the miserable Italian custom-house on the other side. Then began the long descent through snow-galleries and steep pine-forests, above the lonely gorge of the Madesimo: Switzerland still in every aspect, but with a promise of Italy in the names of the dreary villages. Visible Italy began with the valley of the Lira, where, in a wild Salvator Rosa landscape, the beautiful campanile of the Madonna of Gallevaggio rises above embowering walnuts. After that each successive village declared its allegiance more openly. The huddled stone houses disappeared in a wealth of pomegranates and oleanders. Vine-pergolas shaded the doorways, roses and dahlias

overflowed the terraces of rough masonry, and between the walnut-groves there were melon-patches
and fields of maize.

As we approached Chiavenna a thick bloom of heat
lay on the motionless foliage, and the mountains hung
like thunder-clouds on the horizon. There was something oppressive, menacing almost, in the still weight
of the atmosphere. It seemed to have absorbed all
the ardour of the sun-baked Lombard plain, of the
shadeless rice and maize fields stretching away to the
south of us. But the eye had ample compensation.
The familiar town of Chiavenna had grown as fan-
tastically picturesque as the background of a fresco.
The old houses, with their medallioned doorways of
worn marble; the court-yards bright with flowers and
shaded by trellised vines; the white turbulence of the
Lira, rushing between gardens, balconies and terraces set at reckless angles above the water—were all
these a part of the town we had so often seen at less
romantic seasons? The general impression was of an
exuberance of rococo—as though the sportive statue
of Saint John Nepomuc on the bridge, the grotesque
figures on the balustrade of the pale-green villa near

the hotel, and the stucco shrines at the street corners, had burst into a plastic efflorescence rivalling the midsummer wealth of the gardens.

We had left Switzerland with the general object of going to Italy and the specific one of exploring the Bergamasque Alps. It was the name which had attracted us, as much from its intrinsic picturesqueness as from its associations with the *commedia dell'-arte* and the jolly figures of Harlequin and Brighella. I have often journeyed thus in pursuit of a name, and have seldom been unrewarded. In this case the very aspect of the map was promising. The region included in the scattered lettering—*Bergamasker Hochthäler*—had that furrowed, serried look so encouraging to the experienced traveller. It was rich, crowded, suggestive; and the names of the villages were enchanting.

Early the next morning we set out for Colico, at the head of the Lake of Como, and thence took train for Sondrio, the chief town of the Valtelline. The lake, where we had to wait for our train, lay in unnatural loveliness beneath a breathless sky, the furrowed peaks bathed in subtle colour-gradations of which, at other seasons, the atmosphere gives no hint.

At Sondrio we found all the dreariness of a modern
Italian town with wide unshaded streets; but taking
carriage in the afternoon for Madonna di Tirano we
were soon in the land of romance again. The Valtelline, through which we drove, is one vast fruit and
vegetable garden of extraordinary fertility. The
gran turco (as the maize is called) grows in jungles
taller than a man, and the grapes and melons have
the exaggerated size and bloom of their counterfeits
in a Dutch fruit-piece. The rich dulness of this foreground was relieved by the noble lines of the hills, and
the air cooled by the rush of the Adda, which followed
the windings of our road, and by a glimpse of snow-
peaks at the head of the valley. The villages were
uninteresting, but we passed a low-lying deserted
church, a charming bit of seventeenth-century decay,
with peeling stucco ornaments, and weeds growing
from the florid vases of the pediment; and far off, on
a lonely wooded height, there was a tantalizing
glimpse of another church, a Renaissance building
rich with encrusted marbles: one of the nameless un-
catalogued treasures in which Italy still abounds.

Toward sunset we reached Madonna di Tirano,
the great pilgrimage church of the Valtelline.

With its adjoining monastery it stands alone in poplar-shaded meadows a mile or more from the town of Tirano. The marble church, a late fifteenth-century building by Battagio (the architect of the Incoronata of Lodi), has the peculiar charm of that transitional period when individuality of detail was merged, but not yet lost, in the newly-recovered sense of unity. From the columns of the porch, with their Verona-like arabesques, to the bronze Saint Michael poised like a Mercury on the cupola, the whole building combines the charm and naïveté of the earlier tradition with the dignity of a studied whole. The interior, if less homogeneous, is, in the French sense, even more "amusing." Owing, doubtless, to the remote situation of the church, it has escaped the unifying hand of the improver, and presents three centuries of conflicting decorative treatment, ranging from the marble chapel of the Madonna, so suggestive, in its clear-edged reliefs, of the work of Omodeo at Pavia, to the barocco carvings of the organ and the eighteenth-century *grisailles* beneath the choir-gallery.

The neighbouring monastery of Saint Michael has been turned into an inn without farther change than that of substituting tourists for monks in the white-washed cells around the cloisters. The old building is a dusty labyrinth of court-yards, loggias and pigeon-haunted upper galleries, which it needs but little imagination to people with cowled figures gliding to lauds or benediction; and the refectory where we supped is still hung with portraits of cardinals, monsignori, and lady abbesses holding little ferret-like dogs.

The next day we drove across the rich meadows to Tirano, one of those unhistoried and unconsidered Italian towns which hold in reserve for the observant eye a treasure of quiet impressions. It is difficult to name any special "effect": the hurried sight-seer may discover only dull streets and featureless house-fronts. But the place has a fine quality of age and aloofness. The featureless houses are "palaces," long-fronted and escutcheoned, with glimpses of arcaded courts, and of gardens where maize and dahlias smother the broken statues and choked fountains, and where grapes ripen on the peeling stucco walls. Here and there one comes on a frivolous rococo church, subdued by time to delicious harmony with its surroundings; on a fountain in a quiet square, or a wrought-iron balcony projecting romantically from a shuttered façade; or on one or another of the hundred characteristic details which go to make up the *mise en scène* of the average Italian town. It is precisely in places like Tirano, where there are no salient beauties to fix the eye, that one appreciates the value of these details, that one realizes what may be called the negative strength of the Italian artistic sense. Where the Italian builder could not be grand, he could always abstain from being mean and trivial; and this artistic abnegation gives to many a dull little town like Tirano an architectural dignity which our great cities lack.

II

THE return to secular life was made two days later, when we left our monastery and set out to drive across the Aprica pass to Edolo. Retracing for a mile or two the way toward Sondrio, we took a turn to the left and began to mount the hills through forests of beech and chestnut. With each bend of the road the views down the Valtelline toward Sondrio and Como grew wider and more beautiful. No one who has not looked out on such a prospect in the early light of an August morning can appreciate the poetic truth of Claude's interpretation of nature: we seemed to be moving through a gallery hung with his pictures. There was the same expanse of billowy forest, the same silver winding of a river through infinite gradations of distance, the same aërial line of hills melting into illimitable sky.

As we neared the top of the pass the air freshened, and pines and open meadows replaced the forest. We lunched at a little hotel in a bare meadow, among a crowd of Italians enjoying the *villeggiatura* in their shrill gregarious fashion; then we began the descent to Edolo in the Val Camonica.

The scenery changed rapidly as we drove on. There was no longer any great extent of landscape, as on the other side of the pass, but a succession of small park-like views: rounded clumps of trees interspersed with mossy glades, water-falls surmounted by old mills, *campanili* rising above villages hidden in foliage. On these smooth grassy terraces, under the walnut boughs, one expected at each turn to come upon some pastoral of Giorgione's, or on one of Bonifazio's sumptuous picnics. The scenery has a studied beauty in which velvet robes and caparisoned palfreys would not be out of place, and even the villages might have been "brushed in" by an artist skilled in effects and not afraid to improve upon reality.

It was after sunset when we reached Edolo, a dull town splendidly placed at the head of the Val Camonica, beneath the ice-peaks of the Adamello. The Oglio, a loud stream voluble of the glaciers, rushes through the drowsy streets as though impatient to be gone; and we were not sorry, the next morning, to follow its lead and continue our way down the valley.

III

THE Val Camonica, which extends from the Adamello group to the head of the lake of Iseo, is a smaller and more picturesque reproduction of the Valtelline. Vines and maize again fringed our way; but the mountains were closer, the villages more frequent and more picturesque.

We had read in the invaluable guide-book of Gsell-Fels a vague allusion to an interesting church among these mountains, but we could learn nothing of it at Edolo, and only by persistent enquiries along the

E C Peixotto
BRESCIA 190.

road did we finally hear that there *was* a church with "sculptures" in the hill-village of Cerveno, high above the reach of carriages. We left the high-road at the point indicated, and drove in a light country carriole up the stony mule-path, between vines and orchards, till the track grew too rough for wheels; then we continued the ascent on foot. As we approached the cluster of miserable hovels which had been pointed out to us we felt sure we had been misled. Not even in Italy, the land of unsuspected treasures, could one hope to find a church with "sculptures" in a poverty-stricken village on this remote mountain! Cerveno does not even show any signs of past prosperity. It has plainly never been more than it now is—the humblest of *paesi,* huddled away in an unvisited fold of the Alps. The peasants whom we met still insisted that the church we sought was close at hand; but the higher we mounted the lower our anticipations fell.

Then suddenly, at the end of a long stony lane, we came on an imposing doorway. The church to which it belonged stood on a higher ledge of the hill, and the door led into a vaulted ascent, with shallow flights of steps broken by platforms or landings—a small but yet impressive imitation of the Bernini staircase in the Vatican. As we mounted we found that each landing opened into a dimly-lit chapel with grated doors, through which we discerned terra-cotta groups representing the scenes of the Passion. The staircase was in fact a Sacred Way like the more famous one of Varallo; but there was distinct originality in placing the chapels on each side of the long flight of steps leading to the church, instead of scattering them on an open hill-side, according to the traditional plan common to all the other sacred mountains of northern Italy.

The dilettante will always allow for the heightening of emotion that attends any unexpected artistic "find"; but, setting this subjective impression aside, the Via Crucis of Cerveno remains in my memory as among the best examples of its kind—excepting always the remarkable terra-cottas of San Vivaldo in Tuscany. At Cerveno, as at Varallo, the groups are marked by unusual vivacity and expressiveness. The main lines of the composition are conventional, and the chief personages—Christ and the Apostles, the Virgin and the other holy characters—are modelled on traditional types; but the minor figures, evidently taken from life, are rendered with frank realism and with extraordinary truth of expression and gesture. Just such types—the dwarf, the beggar, the hunchback, the brawny waggoner or ploughman—had met us in every village on the way to Cerveno. As in all the hill-regions where the goitre is prevalent, the most villanous characters in the drama are depicted with a hideous bag of flesh beneath the chin; and Signorelli could not have conceived more bestial leering cruelty than that in some of the faces which press about the dying Christ. The scenes follow the usual order of the sacred story, without marked departure from the conventional grouping; but there is unusual pathos in the Descent from the Cross, where the light from the roof of the chapel falls with tragic intensity on the face of a Magdalen full of suave Lombard beauty.

Hardly less surprising than this remarkable stairway is the church to which it leads. The walls are hung with devotional pictures set in the faded gilding of rich old frames, the altar-fronts are remarkable examples of sixteenth-century wood-carving, and the high altar is surmounted by an elaborate tabernacle, also of carved wood, painted and gilt, that in itself repays the effort of the climb to Cerveno. This tabernacle is a complicated architectural composition—like one of the fantastic designs of Fontana or Bibbiena—thronged with tiny saints and doctors, angels and *putti,* akin to the little people of the Neapolitan *presepii:* a celestial company fluttering

Si come schiera d' api che s' infiora

around the divine group which surmounts the shrine.

This prodigality of wood-carving, surprising as it is in so remote and humble a church, is yet characteristic of the region about Brescia and Bergamo. Lamberti of Brescia, the sculptor of the famous frame of Romanino's Madonna in the church of San Francesco, was one of the greatest wood-carvers of the Italian Renaissance; and every church and chapel in the country through which we were travelling bore witness to the continued practice of the art in some graceful frame or altar-front, some saint or angel rudely but expressively modelled.

We lunched that day at Breno, a town guarded by a ruined castle on a hill, and sunset brought us to Lovere, at the head of the lake of Iseo. It was the stillest of still evenings, and the little town which Lady Mary Wortley Montagu has immortalized was reflected, with every seam and wrinkle of its mountain background, in the pearly surface of the lake. Literal-minded critics, seeking in vain along the shore for Lady Mary's villa and garden, have grumbled at the inaccuracy of her descriptions; but every lover of Italy will understand the mental process by which she unconsciously created an imaginary Lovere. For though the town, at first sight, is dull and disappointing, yet, taken with its surroundings, it might well form the substructure of one of those Turneresque visions which, in Italy, are perpetually intruding between the most conscientious traveller and his actual surroundings. It is indeed almost impossible to see Italy steadily and see it whole. The onset of impressions and memories is at times so overwhelming that observation is lost in mere sensation.

Certainly he who, on an August morning, sails from Lovere to Iseo, at the southern end of the lake, is likely to find himself succumbing to Lady Mary's hallucinations. Warned by her example, and conscious of lacking her extenuating gift, I hesitate to record my impressions of the scene; or venture, at most, to do so in the past tense, asserting (and this even with a mental reservation) that on a certain morning a certain number of years ago the lake of Iseo wore such and such an aspect. But the difficulty of rendering the aspect remains. I can only say it was that very lake of the *carte du Tendre* upon which, in the eighteenth-century romances, gay parties in velvet-hung barges used to set out for the island of Cythera. Every village on that enchanted shore might have been the stage of some comedy in the Bergamasque dialect, with Harlequin in striped cloak, and Brighella in conical hat and wide green and white trousers, strutting up and down before the shuttered house in which Dr. Graziano hides his pretty ward; every villa reflecting its awnings and bright flowers in the lake might have housed some Rosaura to whom Leandro, the Tuscan lover, warbled *rispetti* beneath the padlocked water-gate; every pink or yellow monastery on the hill-side might have sent forth its plausible friar, descendant of Macchiavelli's Fra Timoteo, to preach in the market-place, beg at the villa-door, and help Rosaura and Leandro cozen the fat dupe of a Pantaloon in black cloak and scarlet socks. The eighteenth century of

Longhi, of Tiepolo and Goldoni was reflected in the lake ás in some magic crystal. Did the vision dissolve as we landed at Iseo, or will some later traveller find it still lying beneath the wave like the vanished city of Ys? There is no telling, in such cases, how much the eye receives and how much it contributes; and if ever the boundaries between fact and fancy waver, it may well be under the spell of the Italian midsummer madness.

IV

THE sun lay heavy on Iseo; and the railway journey thence to Brescia left in our brains a golden dazzle of heat. It was refreshing, on reaching Brescia, to enter the streets of the old town, where the roofs almost meet and there is always a blessed strip of shade to walk in. The cities in Italy are much cooler than the country. It is in August that one understands the wisdom of the old builders, who made the streets so narrow, and built dim draughty arcades around the open squares. In Brescia the effects of light and shade thus produced were almost Oriental in their sharp-edged intensity; the rough stucco surfaces gilded with vivid sunlight bringing out the depths of

contrasting shade, and the women with black veils
over their heads slipping along under the mysterious
balconies and porticoes like flitting fragments of the
shadow.

Brescia is at all times a delightful place to linger
in. Its chief possessions—the bronze Victory, and
that room in the Martinengo palace where Moretto,
in his happiest mood, depicted the ladies of the line
under arches of trellis-work backed by views of the
family villas—make it noteworthy even among Italian cities; and it has, besides, its beautiful town-hall,
its picture-gallery, and the curious court-yards
painted in perspective that are so characteristic of
the place. But in summer there is a strong tempta-
tion to sit and think of these things rather than to
go and see them. In the court-yard of the hotel,
where a fountain tinkles refreshingly, and the un-
bleached awnings flap in the breeze of the electric
fans, it is pleasant to feel that the Victory and the
pictures are close at hand, like old friends waiting on
one's inclination; but if one ventures forth, let it be
rather to the churches than to the galleries. Only at
this season can one appreciate the atmosphere of the
churches: that chill which cuts the sunshine like a
knife as one steps across the dusky threshold. When

we entered the cathedral its vast aisles were empty, but far off, in the dimness of the pillared choir, we heard a drone of intoning canons that freshened the air like the sound of a water-fall in a forest. Thence we wandered on to San Francesco, empty too, where, in the sun-spangled dimness, the great Romanino throned behind the high altar. The sacristan drew back the curtain before the picture, and as it was revealed to us in all its sun-bathed glory he exclaimed with sudden wonder, as though he had never seen it before: *"È stupendo! È stupendo!"* Perhaps he vaguely felt, as we did, that Romanino, to be appreciated, must be seen in just that light, a projection of the suave and radiant atmosphere in which his own creations move. Certainly no Romanino of the great public galleries arrests the imagination like the Madonna of San Francesco; and in its presence one thinks with a pang of all the beautiful objects uprooted from their native soil to adorn the herbarium of the art-collector. . . .

V

IT was on the last day of our journey that the most imperturbable member of the party, looking up from a prolonged study of the guide-books, announced that we had not seen the Bergamasque Alps after all.

In the excited argument that followed, proof seemed to preponderate first on one side and then on the other; but a closer scrutiny of the map confirmed the fear that we had not actually penetrated beyond the borders of the promised land. It must be owned that at first the discovery was somewhat humiliating; but on reflection it left us overjoyed to think that we had still the Bergamasque Alps to visit. Meanwhile our pleasure had certainly been enhanced by our delusion; and we remembered with fresh admiration Goethe's profound saying—a saying which Italy inspired—

O, wie beseliget uns Menschen ein falscher Begriff!

THE SANCTUARIES OF THE
PENNINE ALPS

THE SANCTUARIES OF THE
PENNINE ALPS

WHEN June is hot on the long yellow
streets of Turin, it is pleasant to take
train for the Biellese, that romantic hill-
country where the last slopes of the Pennine Alps
melt into the Piedmontese plain.

The line, crossing the lowland with its red-tiled
farm-houses and mulberry orchards, rises gradually
to a region of rustling verdure. Mountain streams
flow down between alder-fringed banks, white oxen
doze under the acacia-hedges, and in the almond and
cherry orchards the vine hangs its Virgilian garlands
from blossoming tree to tree. This pastoral land
rolls westward to the Graiian Alps in an undulating
sea of green, but to the north it breaks abruptly into
the height against which rises the terraced outline of
Biella.

The cliffs of the Biellese are the haunt of ancient legend, and on almost every ledge a church or monastery perpetuates the story of some wonder-working relic. Biella, the chief town of this devout district, covers a small conical hill and spreads its suburbs over the surrounding level. Its hot sociable streets are full of the shrill activity of an Italian watering-place; but the transalpine traveller will probably be inclined to push on at once to the village of Andorno, an hour's drive deeper in the hills.

Biella overhangs the plain; but Andorno lies in a valley which soon contracts to a defile between the mountains. The drive thither from Biella skirts the Cervo, a fresh mountain stream, and passes through villages set on park-like slopes in the ample shade of chestnut-groves. The houses of these villages have little of the picturesqueness mistakenly associated with Italian rural architecture; but every window displays its pot of lavender or of carnations, and the arched doorways reveal gardens flecked with the blue shadows of the vine-pergola.

Andorno itself is folded in hills, rounded, umbrageous, cooled with the song of birds. A sylvan hush envelops the place, and the air one breathes

seems to have travelled over miles of forest freshened
by unseen streams. It is all as still and drowsy as
the dream of a tired brain. There is nothing to see
but the country itself—acacia-fringed banks sloping
to the stream below the village; the arch of a ruined
bridge; an old hexagonal chapel with red-tiled roof
and an arcade of stunted columns; and, beyond the
bridge and the chapel, rich upland meadows where all
day long the peasant women stoop to the swing of the
scythe.

In June in this high country (where patches of
snow still lie in the shaded hollows), the wild flowers
of spring and summer seem to meet: narcissus and
forget-me-not lingering in the grass, while yellow
broom—Leopardi's *lover of sad solitudes*—sheets the
dry banks with gold, and higher up, in the folds of
the hills, patches of crimson azalea mix their shy scent
with the heavy fragrance of the acacia. In the meadows the trees stand in well-spaced majestic groups,
walnut, chestnut and beech, tenting the grass with
shade. The ivy hangs its drapery over garden walls
and terraces, and the streams rush down under a
quivering canopy of laburnum. The scenery of these
high Pennine valleys is everywhere marked by the

same nobleness of colour and outline, the same atmosphere of spaciousness and poetry. It is the rich studied landscape of Bonifazio's idyls: a scene of peace and plenitude, not the high-coloured southern opulence but the sober wealth poured from a glacial horn of plenty. There is none of the Swiss abruptness, of the Swiss accumulation of effects. The southern aspect softens and expands. There is no crowding of impressions, but a stealing sense of harmony and completeness.

From Andorno the obvious excursion is to the famous shrine of San Giovanni; a "sight" taking up eight pages in the excellent "Guida del Biellese," but remaining in the traveller's memory chiefly as the objective point of a charming walk or drive. The road thither winds up the Val d'Andorno, between heights set with villages hung aloft among the beech-groves, or thrusting their garden-parapets above the spray and tumult of the Cervo. The densely-wooded cliffs are scarred with quarries of sienite, and the stream, as the valley narrows, forces its way over masses of rock and between shelving stony banks; but the little gardens dashed by its foam overflow with irises, roses and peonies, surrounded with box-hedges and shaded by the long mauve panicles of the wistaria.

Presently the road leaves the valley, and ascends the beech-clothed flank of the mountain on which the church of San Giovanni is perched. The coolness and hush of this wooded hill-side are delicious after the noise and sunshine of the open road, and one is struck by the civic amenity which, in this remote soli-tude, has placed benches at intervals beneath the trees. At length the brow of the hill is reached. The beeches recede, leaving a grassy plateau flanked by a long façade of the monastery; and from the brink of this open space the eye drops unhindered down the long leafy reaches of the Val d'Andorno.

The scene is characterized by the tenderest grada-tions of colour and line: beeches blending with wal-nuts, these with the tremulous laburnum-thickets along the stream, and the curves of the hills flowing into one another till they lose themselves in the aërial distances of the plain. The building which com-mands this outlook is hardly worthy of its station, unless, indeed, the traveller feels its sober lines to be an admission of art's inferiority to nature in such as-pects. To the confirmed apologist of Italy there is indeed a certain charm in finding so insignificant a piece of architecture in so rare a spot: as though in a land thus amply dowered no architectural emphasis were needed to call attention to any special point of view. Yet a tenderness for the view, one cannot but infer, must have guided the steps of those early ceno-bites who peopled the romantic landscape with won-der-working images. When did a miracle take place on a barren plain or in a circumscribed hollow? The manifestations of divine favour invariably sought the heights, and those who dedicated themselves to the commemoration of such holy incidents did so in surroundings poetic enough to justify their faith in the supernatural.

The church, with its dignified front and sculptured portal, adjoins the hospice, and shows little of interest within but the stone grotto containing the venerated image of Saint John, discovered in the third century by Saint Eusebius, Bishop of Vercelli. This grotto is protected by an iron grating, and its dark recess twin-kles with silver hearts and other votive offerings. The place is still a favourite pilgrimage, but there seems to be some doubt as to which Saint John has chosen it as the scene of his posthumous thaumaturgy; for, ac-

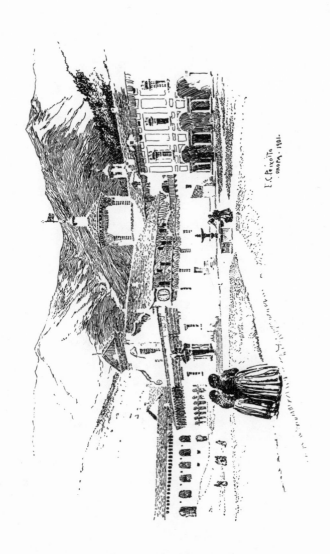

cording to the local guide-book, it is equally fre-
quented on the feasts of the Baptist and of the Evan-
gelist. This uncertainty is not without its practical
advantages; and one reads that the hospice is open
the year round, and that an excellent meal may always be enjoyed in the *trattoria* above the arcade;
while on the feasts of the respective saints it is necessary for the devotee to bespeak his board and lodging
in advance.

If San Giovanni appeals chiefly to the lover of
landscape, the more famous sanctuary of Oropa is
of special interest to the architect; for thither, in the
eighteenth century, the piety of the house of Savoy
sent Juvara, one of the greatest architects of his time,
to add a grand façade and portico to the group of
monastic buildings erected a hundred years earlier by
Negro di Pralungo.

The ascent to the great mountain-shrine of the
Black Virgin leads the traveller back to Biella, and
up the hills behind the town. The drive is long, but
so diversified, so abounding in beauty, that in near-
ing its end one feels the need of an impressive monument to close so nobly ordered an approach. As the
road rises above the vineyards of Biella, as the house-

roofs, the church-steeples and the last suburban villas drop below the line of vision, there breaks upon the eye the vast undulating reach of the Piedmontese plain. From the near massing of cultivated verdure —the orchards, gardens, groves of the minutely pencilled foreground—to the far limit where earth and sky converge in silver, the landscape glides through every gradation of sun-lit cloud-swept loveliness. First the Val d'Andorno unbosoms its wooded depths; then the distances press nearer, blue-green and dappled with forest, with the towns of Biella, Novara and Vercelli like white fleets anchored on a misty sea. This view, with its fold on fold of woodland, dusky-shimmering in the foreground, then dark blue, with dashes of tawny sunlight and purple streaks of rain, till it fades into the indeterminate light of the horizon, suggests some heroic landscape of Poussin's, or the boundless russet distances of Rubens's " Château of Stein."

Meanwhile the foreground is perpetually changing. The air freshens, the villages with their flower-gardens and their guardian images of the Black Virgin are left behind, and between the thinly-leaved beeches rise bare gravelly slopes backed by treeless hills. The Loreto of Piedmont lies nearly four thousand feet above the sea, and even in June there is a touch of snow in the air. For a moment one fancies one's self in Switzerland; but here, at the bend of the road, is a white chapel with a classic porch, within which a group of terra-cotta figures enact some episode of the Passion. Italy has reasserted herself and art has humanized the landscape. More chapels are scattered through the trees, but one forgets to note them as the carriage turns into a wide grassy forecourt, bordered by stone pyramids and dominated at its farther end by the great colonnade of the hospice. A *rampe douce* with fine iron gates leads up to an outer court enclosed in the arcaded wings of the building. Under these arcades are to be found shops in which the pilgrim may satisfy his various wants, from groceries, wines and cotton umbrellas (much needed in these showery hills), to rosaries, images of the Black Virgin, and pious histories of her miracles. Above the arcades the pilgrims are lodged; and in the centre of the inner façade Juvara's marble portico unfolds its double flight of steps.

Passing through this gateway, one stands in a spacious inner quadrangle. This again is enclosed in low buildings resting on arcades, their alignment broken only by the modest façade of the church. Outside there is the profane bustle of life, the clatter of glasses at the doors of rival *trattorie,* the cracking of whips, the stir of buying and selling; but a warm silence holds the inner court. Only a few old peasant women are hobbling, rosary in hand, over the sun-baked flags to the cool shelter of the church. The church is indeed cavernously cold, with that subter-ranean chill peculiar to religious buildings. The in-terior is smaller and plainer than one had expected; but presently it is seen to be covered with a decoration beside which the rarest tapestry or fresco might sink into insignificance. This covering is composed of in-numerable votive offerings, crowding each other from floor to vaulting over every inch of wall, light-ing the chapels with a shimmer of silver and tinsel, with the yellow of old wax legs and arms, and the gleam of tarnished picture-frames: each overlapping scale of this strange sheath symbolizing some impulse of longing, grief or gratitude, so that, as it were, the whole church is lined with heart-beats. Most of these offerings are the gift of the poor mountain-folk, and the paintings record with artless realism the miraculous escapes of carters, quarrymen and stone-cutters. In the choir, however, hang a few portraits of noble donators in ruffs and Spanish jerkins; and one picture, rudely painted on the wall itself, renders with touching fidelity the interior of a peasant's house in the sixteenth or seventeenth century, with the mother kneeling by a cradle over which the Black Virgin sheds her reassuring light.

The ebony Virgin herself (another " find " of the indefatigable Saint Eusebius) is enthroned behind the high altar, in a tiny chapel built by her discoverer, where, in a blaze of altar-lights, the miraculous image, nimbused in jewels and gold, showers a dazzling brightness on the groups who succeed each other at her iron lattice. The incense-laden air and the sweating stone walls encrusted with votive offerings recall at once the chapel of Loreto; but here the smaller space, the deeper dusk, heighten the sense of holiness and solemnity; and if a few white-capped Sisters are grouped against the grating, while before the altar a sweet-voiced young priest intones the mystic

Mater purissima,
Mater admirabile,
Mater prudentissima,

[51]

punctuated by the wailing *Ora pro nobis!* of the nuns, it would be hard to picture a scene richer in that mingling of suavity and awe with which the Church composes her incomparable effects.

After so complex an impression the pleasures of the eye may seem a trifle thin; yet there is a great charm in the shaded walks winding through the colony of chapels above the monastery. Nothing in nature is lovelier than a beech-wood rustling with streams; and to come, in such a setting, on one graceful *tempietto* after another, to discover, in their semi-pagan porches, groups of peasants praying before some dim presentment of the Passion, gives a renewed sense of the way in which, in Italy, nature, art and religion combine to enrich the humblest lives. These Sacred Mounts, or Stations of the Cross, are scattered everywhere on the Italian slopes of the Alps. The most famous is at Varallo, and to find any artistic merit one must go there, or to San Vivaldo in Tuscany, or the unknown hill-village of Cerveno in the Val Camonica. At Oropa the groups are relatively crude and uninteresting; but the mysterious half-light in which they are seen, and the surrounding murmur of leaves and water, give them a value quite independent of their plastic qualities.

VARALLO itself is but a day's journey from Andorno, and in June weather the drive thither is beautiful. The narrow country road mounts through chestnut-groves as fine as those which cast their velvet shade for miles about Promontogno in the Val Bregaglia. At first the way dips continuously from one green ravine to another, but at Mosso Santa Maria, the highest point of the ascent, the glorious plain again bursts into view, with white roads winding toward distant cities, and the near flanks of the hills clothed in unbroken forest. The Val Sesia is broader than the Val d'Andorno, and proportionately less pictur-esque; but its expanse of wheat and vine, checkered with shade and overhung by piled-up mossy rocks, offers a restful contrast to the landscape of the higher valleys. As Varallo is neared the hills close in again and the scenery regains its sub-Alpine char-acter. The first unforgettable glimpse of the old town is caught suddenly at a bend of the road, with the Sanctuary lifted high above the river, and tiled roofs and church-towers clustered at its base. The near approach is a disenchantment; for few towns have suffered more than Varallo under the knife of "modern improvement," and those who did not know it in earlier days would hardly guess that it was once the most picturesque town in North Italy. A dusty wide-avenued suburb, thinly scattered with cheap villas, now leads from the station to the edge of the old town; and the beautiful slope facing the Sacred Mountain has been cleared of its natural growth and planted with moribund palms and camellias, to form the "pleasure" grounds of a huge stucco hotel with failure written over every inch of its pretentious façade.

One knows not whether to lament the impairment of such rare completeness, or to find consolation in the fact that Varallo is rich enough not to be ruined by its losses. Ten or fifteen years ago every aspect was enchanting; now one must choose one's point of view, but one or two of the finest are still intact. Turning one's back, for instance, on the offending hotel, one has still, on a summer morning, the rarest vision of wood and water and happily-blended architecture: the Sesia with its soft meadows and leafy banks, the old houses huddled above it, and the high cliff crowned by the chapels of the Sacred Way. At night all melts to a diviner loveliness. The clustered darkness of the town, twinkling with lights, lies folded in hills delicately traced against a sky mauve with moonlight. Here and there the moon burnishes a sombre mass of trees, or makes a campanile stand out pale and definite as ivory; while high above, the summit of the cliff projects against the sky, with an almost Greek purity of outline, the white domes and arches of the Sanctuary.

The centre of the town is also undisturbed. Here one may wander through cool narrow streets with shops full of devotional emblems, and of the tall votive candles gaily spangled with gold, and painted with flower-wreaths and *mandorle* of the Virgin. These streets, on Sundays, are thronged with the peasant women of the neighbouring valleys in their various costumes: some with cloth leggings and short dark-blue cloth petticoats embroidered in colours; others in skirts of plaited black silk, with embroidered jackets, silver necklaces and spreading head-dresses; for nearly every town has its distinctive dress, and some happy accident seems to have preserved this slope of the Alps from the depressing uniformity of modern fashions. In architectural effects the town is little richer than its neighbours; but it has that indescribable "tone" in which the soft texture of old stucco and the bloom of weather-beaten marble combine with a hundred happy accidents of sun and shade to produce what might be called the *patine* of Italy. There is, indeed, one remarkable church, with a high double flight of steps leading to its door; but this (though it contains a fine Gaudenzio) passes as a mere incident in the general picturesqueness, and the only church with which the sight-seer seriously reckons is that of Santa Maria delle Grazie, frescoed with the artist's scenes from the Passion.

There is much beauty of detail in these crowded compositions; but, to the inexpert, Gaudenzio lives perhaps chiefly as the painter of the choiring angels of Saronno: so great there that elsewhere he seems relatively unimportant. At Varallo, at least, one associates him first with the Sacred Mountain. To this great monument of his native valley he contributed some of his most memorable work, and it seems fitting that on turning from his frescoes in Santa Maria one should find one's self at the foot of the path leading to the Sanctuary. The wide approach, paved

E C Peixotto
Varallo 1901

with tiny round pebbles polished by the feet of thousands of pilgrims, leads round the flank of the cliff to the park-like enclosure on its summit. Here, on the ledge overlooking the town, stands the church built by Saint Charles Borromeo (now disfigured by a modern façade), and grouped about it are the forty-two chapels of the "New Jerusalem." These little buildings, to which one mounts or descends by mossy winding paths beneath the trees, present every variety of pseudo-classical design. Some, placed at different levels, are connected by open colonnades and long flights of steps; some have airy loggias, overlooking gardens tufted with blush-roses and the lilac iris; while others stand withdrawn in the deep shade of the beeches. Each chapel contains a terra-cotta group representing some scene in the divine history, and the site and architecture of each building have been determined by a subtle sense of dramatic fitness. Thus, the chapels enclosing the earlier episodes—the Annunciation, the Nativity and the scenes previous to the Last Supper—are placed in relatively open sites, with patches of flowers about their door-steps; while as the drama darkens the pilgrim descends into deep shady hollows, or winds along chill stone corridors and up and down interminable stairs; a dark subterranean passage leading at last to the image of the buried Christ.

Of the groups themselves it is difficult to speak dispassionately, for they are so much a part of their surroundings that one can hardly measure them by any conventional standard. To do so, indeed, would be to miss their meaning. They must be studied as a reflection of the Bible story in the hearts of simple and emotional peasants; for it was the piety of the mountain-folk that called them into being, and the modellers and painters who contributed to the work were mostly natives of Val Sesia or of the neighbouring valleys. The art of clay modelling is peculiarly adapted to the rendering of strong and direct emotions. So much vivacity of expression do its rapid evocations permit, that one might almost describe it as intermediate between pantomime and sculpture. The groups at Varallo have the defects inherent in such an improvisation: the crudeness, the violence, sometimes even the seeming absurdities of an instantaneous photograph. These faults are redeemed by a simplicity and realism which have not had time to harden into conventionality. The Virgin and Saint

Elizabeth are low-browed full-statured peasant
women; the round-cheeked romping children, the
dwarfs and hunchbacks, the Roman soldiers and the
Jewish priests, have all been transferred alive from
the market-places of Borgo Sesia and Arona. These
expressive figures, dressed in real clothes, with real
hair flowing about their shoulders, seem like the
actors in some miracle-play arrested at its crowning
moment.

Closer inspection brings to light a marked differ-
ence in quality between the different groups. Those
by Tabacchetti and Fermo Stella are the best, excepting only the remarkable scene of the Crucifixion,
attributed to Gaudenzio, and probably executed from
his design. Tabacchetti is the artist of the Adam and
Eve surrounded by the supra-terrestrial flora and
fauna of Eden: a curious composition, with a golden-
haired Eve of mincing elegance and refinement. To
Stella are due some of the simplest and most moving
scenes of the series: the Adoration of the Magi, the
message of the angel to Joseph, and Christ and the
woman of Samaria. Especially charming is the Annunciation, where a yellow-wigged angel, in a kind
of celestial dressing-gown of flowered brocade, ad-

vances, lily in hand, toward a gracefully-startled Virgin, dressed (as one is told) in a costume presented by a pious lady of Varallo. In another scene the Mother of God, habited like a peasant of Val Sesia, looks up smilingly from the lace-cushion on which she is at work; while the Last Supper, probably a survival of the older wooden groups existing before Gaudenzio and his school took up the work, shows a lace-trimmed linen table-cloth, with bread and fruit set out on real Faenza dishes.

After these homely details the scenes of the Passion, where Gaudenzio's influence probably prevailed, seem a trifle academic; but even here there are local touches, such as the curly white dog at the foot of Herod's throne, the rags of the beggars, the child in the Crucifixion holding a spotted hound in leash.

The Crucifixion is fitly the culminating point of the series. Here Gaudenzio lined the background with one of his noblest frescoes, and the figures placed before it are worthy, in expression and attitude, to carry out the master's conception. The gold-bucklered Roman knight on his white charger, the eager gaping throng, where beggars and cripples jostle turbaned fine ladies and their dwarfs, where oval-faced Lombard women with children at the breast press forward to catch a glimpse of the dying Christ, while the hideous soldiers at the foot of the cross draw lots for the seamless garment—all these crowding careless figures bring out with strange intensity the agony uplifted in their midst. Never, perhaps, has the popular, the unimpressed, unrepentant side of the scene been set forth with more tragic directness. One can fancy the gold-armoured knight echoing in after years the musing words of Anatole France's *Procurateur de Judée:*—"Jésus? Jésus de Nazareth? Je ne me rappelle pas."

FROM Varallo the fortunate traveller may carry his impressions unimpaired through the chestnut-woods and across the hills to the lake of Orta—a small sheet of water enclosed in richest verdure, with the wooded island of San Giuliano on its bosom. Orta has a secret charm of its own: a quality of solitude, of remoteness, that makes it seem the special property of each traveller who chances to discover it. Here too is a Sacred Way, surmounting the usual knoll above the town. The groups have little artistic merit, but there is a solemn charm in the tranquil glades, with their little white-pillared shrines, connected by grass-walks under a continuous vaulting of branches. The chief "feature" of Orta, however, is the incredibly complete little island, with its ancient church embosomed in gardens; yet even this counts only as a detail in the general composition, a last touch to the prodigal picturesqueness of the place. The lake itself is begirt by vine-clad slopes, and in every direction roads and bridle-paths lead across the wooded hills, through glades sheeted in spring-time with primroses and lilies-of-the-valley, to the deeper forest-recesses at the foot of the high Alps.

In any other country the departure from such perfect loveliness must lead to an anti-climax; but there is no limit to the prodigality of the Italian landscape, and the wanderer who turns eastward from Orta may pass through scenes of undiminished beauty till, toward sunset, the hills divide to show Lake Maggiore at his feet, with the Isola Bella moored like a fantastic pleasure-craft upon its waters.

WHAT THE HERMITS SAW

WHAT THE HERMITS SAW

I N almost every gallery of Italy there hangs, among the pictures of the earlier period, one which represents, with loving minuteness of topographical detail, a rocky mountain-side honeycombed with caves and inhabited by hermits.

As a rule, the landscape is comprehensive enough to include the whole Thebaid, with the river at the base of the cliff, the *selva oscura* " fledging the wild-ridged mountain steep by steep," and the various little edifices—huts, chapels and bridges—with which the colony of anchorites have humanized their wild domain. This presentment of the life of the solitaries always remained a favourite subject in Italian art, and even in the rococo period, when piety had become a drawing-room accomplishment, the traditional charm of the " life apart " was commemorated by the mock " hermitages " to be found in every nobleman's park, or by such frescoes as adorn the

entrance to the chapel of the Villa Chigi, near Rome:
a tiny room painted to represent a rocky cleft in the
mountains, with anchorites visiting each other in
their caves, or engaged in the duties of their sylvan
existence.

A vast body of literature—and of a literature peculiarly accessible to the people—has kept alive in
Catholic countries the image of the early solitary.
The Golden Legend, the great Bollandist compila-
tions, and many other collections of pious anecdote,
preserve, in simple and almost childish form, the
names and deeds of the desert saints. In the traditions of the Latin race there still lingers, no doubt, a
sub-conscious memory of the dark days when all
that was gentle and merciful and humane turned to
the desert to escape the desolation of the country
and the foulness of the town. From war and slavery
and famine, from the strife of the circus factions and
the incredible vices and treacheries of civilized life,
the disenchanted Christian, aghast at the more than
pagan corruption of a converted world, fled into the
waste places to wear out his life in penance. The
horrors he left behind surpassed anything the desert
could show—surpassed even the terrors that walked

by night, the airy tongues that syllabled men's names, the lemurs, succubi and painted demons of the tombs. Nevertheless the lives of the early anchorites, who took refuge in the burning solitudes of Egypt and Asia Minor, were full of fears and anguish. Their history echoes with the groans and lamentations of souls in pain, and had their lives been recorded by contemporary artists, the presentment must have recalled those horribly circumstantial studies of everlasting torment which admonished the mediæval worshipper from the walls of every church.

But when Italian art began to chronicle the history of the desert fathers, a change had passed over the spirit of Christianity. If the world was still a dark place, full of fears and evil, solitary communion with God had ceased to become a more dreadful alternative; and when men went forth into the desert they found Christ there rather than the devil. So at least one infers from the spirit in which the Italian painters rendered the life of the Thebaid—transposing its scenes from the parched African desert to their own fertile landscape, and infusing into the lives of the desert fathers that sense of human fellowship with which Saint Francis had penetrated the mediæval conception of Christianity. The first hermits shunned each other as they shunned the image of evil; every human relation was a snare, and they sought each other out only in moments of moral or physical extremity, when flesh or spirit quailed before the hallucinations of solitude. But in the Italian pictures the hermits move in an atmosphere of fraternal tenderness. Though they still lead the "life apart," it is shorn of its grimness and mitigated by acts of friendly ministry and innocent childlike intercourse. The solitaries still dwell in remote inaccessible regions, and for the most part their lives are spent alone; but on the feasts of the Church they visit each other, and when they go on pilgrimage they pause at each other's thresholds.

Yet, though one feels that this new spirit has tamed the desert, and transplanted to it enough of the leaven of human intercourse to exorcise its evil spirits, the imagination remains chiefly struck by the strangeness of the conditions in which these voluntary exiles must have found themselves. The hermits brought little with them from the world of cities and men compared to what they found in the wilderness. Their relation to the earth—their ancient mysterious mother—must have been the most intimate as well as the most interesting part of their lives; as a "return to nature" the experience had a freshness and intensity which the modern seeker after primeval sensations can never hope to recover. For in those days, when distances were measured by the pilgrim's sandal or the ass's hoof, a few miles meant exile, and the mountain visible from the walls of his native town offered the solitary as complete an isolation as the slopes of Lebanon. News travelled at the same pace, when it did not drop by the way. There was little security outside the city walls, and small incentive for the traveller, except from devotional motives, to seek out the anchorite on his inaccessible height.

The hermit, therefore, was thrown back on the companionship of the wild; and what he won from it we read in the gentler legends of the desert, and in the records of the early Italian artists. Much, for instance, is told of the delightful nature of the intercourse between the solitaries and wild animals. The lion having been the typical "denizen" of the Libyan sands, the Italian painter has transplanted him to the Umbrian hill-sides, where, jointly with the wolf and the stag, he lives in gentle community with the an-

chorites. For instead of fleeing from or fighting
these lords of the wilderness, the wise hermits at once
entered into negotiations with them—negotiations
sometimes resulting in life-long friendships, and
sealed by the self-sacrificing death of the adoring
animal. It was of course the power of the cross
which subjugated these savage beasts; and many in-
stances are recorded of the control exercised over wild
animals, and the contrition awakened in them, by the
conquering sign. But the hermits, not content with
asserting their spiritual predominance over these
poor soulless creatures (*non sono Cristiani*), seemed
to feel that such a victory was too easy, and were
themselves won over by the devotion of their dumb
friends, and drawn into a brotherly commerce which
no law of the Church prescribed.

The mystical natural history of the first Christian
centuries facilitated the belief in this intercourse between man and beast. When even familiar domestic
animals were credited with strange symbolic attributes, it was natural to people the wild with the
dragon, the hydra and the cocatrix; to believe that
the young of the elephant were engendered by their
mothers' eating of the mandragora which grows on a

mount near Paradise; that those of the lion were born
dead and resuscitated by their parents' breath; and
that the old eagle renewed his youth by plunging
three times in a magic fountain. It is not strange
that creatures so marvellously endowed should have
entered into friendly relations with the human in-
truders upon their solitude, and subdued their savage
natures to the teachings of their new masters. And
as the lion and the wolf were gradually transformed
into humble but wise companions, so the other influences of the wilderness came to acquire a power over
the solitaries. Even after the early Thebaids had
been gathered in under one or another of the great
monastic rules, seekers after holiness continued to
flee the communal life, and in Italy every lonely
height came to have its recluse. It was impossible
that these little restricted human lives, going forth
singly into the desert, should not be gradually absorbed into it and saturated with its spirit. Think
what a soul-shattering or soul-making experience it
must have been to the dweller in the narrow walled
town or the narrower monastery, to go forth alone,
beyond the ploughed fields and the road to the next
village, beyond the haunts of men and hail of friendly

voices, forth into the unmapped region of hills and forests, where wild beasts and robbers, and other presences less definable but more baleful, lay in wait for the lonely traveller! From robbers there was not much to fear: the solitaries were poor, and it was a great sin to lay hands on them. The wild beasts, too, might be won over to Christian amity; but what of those other presences of which the returning traveller whispered over the evening fire?

At first, no doubt, the feeling of awe was uppermost, and only the heart inflated with divine love could sustain the assaults of fear and loneliness; but gradually, as the noise of cities died out, as the ear became inured to the vast hush of nature, and the mind to the delicious recurrence of untroubled hours —then, wonderfully, imperceptibly, the spirit of the hermit must have put forth tendrils of sympathy and intelligence toward the mysterious world about him. Think of the joy of escaping from the ceaseless brawls, the dirt, disease and misery of the mediæval town, or from the bickering, the tale-bearing, the mechanical devotions of the crowded monastery! Think of the wonder of entering, alone and undisturbed, into communion with this vast still world of cliff and cataract, of bird and beast and flower!

There were, of course, different kinds of hermits: the dull kind whose only object was to escape from the turmoil and rivalry of the city, or the toil and floggings of the farm, and to live drowsily in a warm cleft of the rocks (not too far from the other solitaries), high above the populous plain alternately harried by war and pestilence; and there was the ecstatic, so filled with the immanent light that he saw neither cliff nor cataract, that the various face of nature was no more to him than a window of clear glass opening on the brightness of the beatific vision. But there must have been a third kind also—the kind in whom the divine love, instead of burning like a cold inward flame, overflowed on the whole world about him; to whom, in this new immediate contact with nature, the swallow became a sister, the wolf a brother, the very clods "lovers and lamps": mute Saint Francises, born out of their due time, to whom the life of nature revealed, inarticulately but profoundly, the bond of brotherhood between man and the soil.

It was to these solitaries that the wilderness truly confessed itself, yielding up once more all the terror and the poetry of its ancient life. For the cliffs and forests shunned of men had not always been thus deserted, and always there had throbbed in them the pulse of that strange intermediate life, between the man and the clod, of which the tradition lingers in all lonely places. The hermits of course knew this: the life of ancient days was still close to them. They knew also that the power of the cross had banished from temple and market-place, from garden, house and vineyard, a throng of tutelary beings on whom the welfare of men had once been thought to depend, but who had now been declared false to their trust, and driven forth to join their brothers of the hills and woods. This knowledge rested on no vague rumours, but on authenticated fact. Were not many of the old temples still standing, some built into the walls of Christian churches, others falling into desecrated ruin on lonely cliff and promontory? And was it not known that in these latter the wraiths of the old gods still reassembled? Many pilgrims and travellers bore witness to the fact. Who had not heard of the Jewish wayfarer, overtaken by night in a lonely country, who sought shelter in a ruined temple of Apollo, and would have been blasted by the god and his attendant demons, had he not (converted by fear) dispelled the unholy rout with the sign of the cross?

A tangle of classic and mediæval traditions, Greek,

Etruscan and Germanic, in which the gods of the
Thessalian glades and the werewolves of northern
forests rode the midnight blast in the *chevauchée* of
a wild Walpurgisnacht, haunted the background of
life in that confused age when "ignorant armies
clashed by night" on the battleground of the awaken-
ing human intelligence. To the citizen hugging the
city walls, this supernatural world was dark with images of sin and fear; but to the dweller in the forest,
bold enough to affront the greater terrors of self-
communion, it must have offered a mitigating sense
of fellowship. That it did so is proved even by some
of the earliest legends. It was not always in forms
of peril and perdition that the banished gods mani-
fested themselves to the votaries of the usurper. To
the dweller in the city they may have come in venge-
ful shape, like the Venus, *tout entière à sa proie at-
tachée,* who held fast to the Christian bridegroom's
ring (though surely here one catches a note of the old
longing); but in their native solitude they seem to
have appeared propitiatingly, with timid proffers of
service, as when Saint Anthony, travelling in search
of a fellow-hermit, was guided on his way, first by a
centaur and then by "a little man with hoofs like a
goat."

For generations indeed, for centuries even in that slow-moving time, the divinities of the old dispensation must have remained more familiar to the simple people than the strange new God of Israel. Often they must have stolen back in the twilight, to surprise and comfort the unlettered toilers who still believed in them, still secretly offered them the dripping honeycomb and bowl of ewe's milk, or hung garlands in the cleft tree which they haunted. To some of these humble hearts, grieving for their old fireside gods, and a little bewildered by the demands of the great forbidding Christ who frowned from the golden heights of the Byzantine apse, the "return to nature" must have been like a coming home to the instinctive endearing ways of childhood. How could they be alarmed by the sight of these old exiled gods, familiars of the hearth and garden; they who had been born to the sense of such presences, to half-human intercourse with beings who linked man to the soil that nurtured him, and the roof beneath which he slept?

Even the most holy and learned men of the first Christian centuries did not question the actual existence of the heathen gods, and the Fathers of the

Church expended volumes of controversy in discussing their origin and their influence on a Christianized world. A strange conflict of opinion waged around this burning question. By the greater number of authorities the old gods were believed to be demons, emanations of the mysterious spirit of evil, himself the Ahriman of the ancient Eastern dualism, who had cleverly smuggled himself into the new Christian creed. Yet the oracles, though usually regarded as the voices of these demons, were always believed in and quoted by the Christian Church, and the history of the dark ages abounds in allusion to the authority of the Sibylline books. While Christian scholarship thus struggled under the spell of the old beliefs, how could the artisan and serf have freed themselves from it? Gradually, indeed, the Church, foreseeing the perils of a divided allegiance, and fearing the baleful loveliness of the old gods, was to transform their myths into Christian legend, and so supply a new throng of anthropomorphic conceptions for minds unable to keep their faith alive on the thin abstractions of the schoolmen. The iconography of the early Church bears witness to the skill with which these adaptations were effected, and the slender young Olympians and their symbols pressed into the service of the new faith; but it was long before the results of this process reached the popular mind, and meanwhile the old gods lived on in simple fellowship with the strange saints and angels.

Through all the middle ages the marvellous did not fail from the earth: it simply receded farther from the centres of life, drawing after it the hearts of the adventurous. The Polo brothers were no doubt clear-sighted practical men while they drove their trade in Venice; but wonders pressed upon them when they set foot in the Great Khan's domains. If an astute Italian prince, who lived till the middle of the fifteenth century with the light of the new humanism flooding his court, could yet, on his travels to the Holy Land and Greece, discover castles inhabited by enchanted snakes, as well as wonder-working shrines of his own creed, how could the simple hearts of the anchorite and solitary remain closed to the old wonders?

Shapes which have once inhabited the imagination of man pass reluctantly out of existence. Centuries of poetic belief had peopled the old world with a race of superhuman beings, and as many centuries would be needed to lay their ghosts. It must be remembered, moreover, that no sudden cataclysm, political or intellectual, marked the introduction of the Christian faith. For three centuries after the sacrifice on Calvary, hardly an allusion to the new god is to be found in the pages of the pagan historians and philosophers. Even after he had led the legions of Constantine to victory, and so won official allegiance throughout the Roman world, no violent change marked the beginning of the new era. For centuries still, men ploughed the same fields with ploughs fashioned on the same lines, kept the same holidays with the same rites, and lived on the same store of accumulated beliefs. And in the hearts of the solitaries these beliefs must have lingered longest. For in fleeing the world they were returning to the native habitations of the old gods. They were nature-spirits every one, sprung from the wave, the cloud, the tree. To the cities they had been borne triumphant by the will of men, and from the cities they might be banished at its behest; but who should drive them from their old stronghold in the breast of nature? Their temples might be re-dedicated to the new god, but none could banish them from the temples not made with

hands. Daylight might deny them, but twilight confessed them still. They made no effort to recover the
supremacy which had been wrested from them: the
gods know when their hour has come. But they lived
on, shrinking back more and more into their primitive
forms, into the vapour, the tree-trunk, the moon-
track on the lonely sea; or revealing themselves, in
wistful fugitive glimpses, to the mortals who had
come to share their forest exile.

In what gentle guise they showed themselves, one
may see in many pictures of the Italian *quattro
cento,* some of whose lesser painters seem to have been
in actual communion with this pale woodland Olympus. The gods they depict are not the shining lords
of the Greek heaven, but half-human, half-sylvan
creatures, shy suppliants for mortal recognition, hov-
ering gently on the verge of evanescence. Robetta,
the Florentine engraver, transferred them to some of
his plates, Luini caught their tender grace in his Sacrifice to Pan and Metamorphosis of Daphne, and
Lorenzo Costa gives a glimpse of their sylvan revels
in the Mythological Scene of the Louvre; but it was
Piero di Cosimo who had the clearest intuition of
them. The gentle furred creature of the Death of
Procris might have been the very faun who showed

Saint Anthony the way; and in all Cosimo's mythological pictures one has the same impression of that intermediate world, the twilight world of the conquered, Christianized, yet still lingering gods, so different from the clear upper air of classic art.

Was it, as the scholars would have us believe, mere lack of book-learning and technical skill that kept the painters of the *quattro cento* spell-bound in this mediæval Olympus? Were these vanishing gods and half-gods merely a clumsy attempt to formulate the classic conception of divinity? But the Pisani had discovered Greek plastic art two centuries earlier; but the uncovered wonders of Rome were being daily drawn and measured by skilful hands; but the silhouettes of the antique temples were still outlined against the skies of Greater Greece! No—these lesser artists were not struggling to embody a half-understood ideal. Kept nearer the soil and closer to the past by the very limitations of their genius, they left to the great masters the task of reconstituting classical antiquity, content to go on painting the gods who still lived in their blood, the gods their own forbears had known in the familiar streets and fields, the fading gods whom the hermits were last to see in the lost recesses of the mountain.

A TUSCAN SHRINE

A TUSCAN SHRINE

O NE of the rarest and most delicate pleasures
of the continental tourist is to circumvent
the compiler of his guide-book. The red
volumes which accompany the traveller through Italy
have so completely anticipated the most whimsical
impulses of their readers that it is now almost impossible to plan a tour of exploration without finding, on reference to them, that their author has already been over the ground, has tested the inns,
measured the kilometres, and distilled from the massive tomes of Kugler, Burckhardt and Morelli a
portable estimate of the local art and architecture.
Even the discovery of incidental lapses scarcely consoles the traveller for the habitual accuracy of his
statements; and the only refuge left from his omnis-
cience lies in approaching the places he describes by
a route which he has not taken.

A TUSCAN SHRINE

Those to whom one of the greatest charms of travel
in over-civilized countries consists in such momentary
escapes from the expected, will still find here and
there, even in Italy, a few miles unmeasured by the
guide-book; and it was to enjoy the brief exhilaration of such a discovery that we stepped out of the
train one morning at Certaldo, determined to find
our way thence to San Vivaldo.

For some months we had been vaguely aware that,
somewhere among the hills between Volterra and the
Arno, there lay an obscure monastery containing a
series of terra-cotta groups which were said to represent the scenes of the Passion. No one in Florence
seemed to know much about them; and many of the
people whom we questioned had never even heard of
San Vivaldo. Professor Enrico Ridolfi, at that time
the director of the Royal Museums at Florence, knew
by hearsay of the existence of the groups, and told
me that there was every reason to accept the local tradition which has always attributed them to Giovanni
Gonnelli, the blind modeller of Gambassi, an obscure
artist of the seventeenth century, much praised by
contemporary authors, but since fallen into merited
oblivion. Professor Ridolfi, however, had never seen

any photographs of the groups, and was not unnaturally disposed to believe that they were of small artistic merit, since Gonnelli worked much later, and in a more debased period of taste, than the modeller of the well-known groups at Varallo. Still, even when the more pretentious kind of Italian sculpture was at its lowest, a spark of its old life smouldered here and there in the improvisations of the *plasticatore,* or stucco modeller; and I hoped to find, in the despised groups of San Vivaldo, something of the coarse naïveté and brutal energy which animate their more famous rivals of Varallo. In this hope we started in search of San Vivaldo; and as the guide-books told us that it could be reached only by way of Castel Fiorentino, we promptly determined to attack it from San Gimignano.

At Certaldo, the birthplace of Boccaccio, where the train left us one April morning, we found an archaic little carriage, with a coachman who entered sympathetically into our plan for eluding our cicerone. He told us that he knew a road which led in about four hours across the mountains from San Gimignano to San Vivaldo; and in his charge we were soon crossing the poplar-fringed Elsa and

climbing the steep ascent to San Gimignano, where
we were to spend the night.

The next morning, before sunrise, the little carriage awaited us at the inn door; and as we dashed
out under the gateway of San Gimignano we felt the
thrill of explorers sighting a new continent. It
seemed, in fact, an unknown world which lay beneath
us in the early light. The hills, so definitely etched
at midday, at sunset so softly modelled, had melted
into a silver sea of which the farthest waves were in-
distinguishably merged in billows of luminous mist.
Only the near foreground retained its precision of
outline, and that too had assumed an air of unreality.
Fields, hedges and cypresses were tipped with an
aureate brightness which recalled the golden ripples
running over the grass in the foreground of Botticelli's "Birth of Venus." The sunshine had the
density of gold-leaf: we seemed to be driving through
the landscape of a missal.

At first we had this magical world to ourselves, but
as the light broadened groups of labourers began to
appear under the olives and between the vines; shep-
herdesses, distaff in hand, drove their flocks along the
roadside, and yokes of white oxen with scarlet fringes

above their meditative eyes moved past us with such solemn deliberateness of step that fancy transformed their brushwood-laden carts into the sacred *carroccio* of the past. Ahead of us the road wound through a district of vineyards and orchards, but to the north and east the panorama of the Tuscan hills unrolled range after range of treeless undulations, outlined one upon the other, as the sun grew high, with the delicately-pencilled minuteness of a mountain background of Sebald Beham's. Behind us the fantastic towers of San Gimignano dominated each bend of the road like some persistent mirage of the desert; to the north lay Castel Fiorentino, and far away other white villages gleamed like fossil shells embedded in the hill-sides.

The elements composing the foreground of such Tuscan scenes are almost always extremely simple— slopes trellised with vine and mulberry, under which the young wheat runs like green flame; stretches of ash-coloured olive orchard; and here and there a farm-house with projecting eaves and open loggia, guarded by its inevitable group of cypresses. These cypresses, with their velvety-textured spires of rusty black, acquire an extraordinary value against the neutral-tinted breadth of the landscape; distributed with the sparing hand with which a practised writer uses his exclamation-points, they seem to emphasize the more intimate meaning of the scene; calling the eye here to a shrine, there to a homestead, or testifying by their mere presence to the lost tradition of some barren knoll. But this significance of detail is one of the chief charms of the mid-Italian landscape. It has none of the purposeless prodigality, the extravagant climaxes, of what is called "fine scenery"; nowhere is there any obvious largesse to the eye; but the very reticence of its delicately-moulded lines, its seeming disdain of facile effects, almost give it the quality of a work of art, make it appear the crowning production of centuries of plastic expression.

For some distance the road from San Gimignano to San Vivaldo winds continuously upward, and our ascent at length brought us to a region where agriculture ceases and the way lies across heathery undulations, with a scant growth of oaks and ilexes in the more sheltered hollows. As we drove on, these copses gave way to stone-pines, and presently we dipped over the yoke of the highest ridge and saw below us another sea of hills, with a bare mountain-

spur rising from it like a scaly monster floating on
the waves, its savage spine bristling with the walls
and towers of Volterra.

For nearly an hour we skirted the edge of this
basin of hills, in sight of the ancient city on its livid
cliff; then we turned into a gentler country, through
woods starred with primroses, with a flash of streams
in the hollows; and presently a murmur of church-
bells reached us through the woodland silence. At
the same moment we caught sight of a brick campanile rising above the trees on a slope just ahead of
us, and our carriage turned from the high-road up
a lane with scattered chapels showing their white
façades through the foliage. This lane, making a
sudden twist, descended abruptly between mossy
banks and brought us out on a grass-plot before a
rectangular monastic building adjoining the church
of which the bells had welcomed us. Here was San
Vivaldo, and the chapels we had passed doubtless
concealed beneath their cupolas "more neat than
solemn" the terra-cottas of which we were in search.

The monastery of San Vivaldo, at one time secu-
larized by the Italian government, has now been restored to the Franciscan order, of which its patron

saint was a member. San Vivaldo was born at San Gimignano in the latter half of the thirteenth century, and after joining in his youth the Tertiary Order of Saint Francis, retired to a hollow chestnut-tree in the forest of Camporeno (the site of the present monastery), in which cramped abode he passed the remainder of his life " in continual macerations and abstinence." After his death the tree which had been sanctified in so unusual a manner became an object of devotion among the neighbouring peasantry, who, when it disappeared, raised on the spot an oratory to the Virgin. It is doubtful, however, if this memorial, which fell gradually into neglect, would have preserved San Vivaldo from oblivion, had not that Senancour of a saint found a Matthew Arnold in the shape of a Franciscan friar, a certain Fra Cherubino of Florence, who, early in the sixteenth century, was commissioned by his order to watch over and restore the abandoned sanctuary. Fra Cherubino, with his companions, took possession of the forest of Camporeno, and proceeded to lay the foundation-stone of a monastery which was to commemorate the hermit of the chestnut-tree. The forgotten merits of San Vivaldo were speedily restored to popular favour by the friar's eloquence, and often, after one of his sermons, three thousand people were to be seen marching in procession to the river Evola to fetch building-materials for the monastery. Meanwhile Fra Tommaso, another of the monks, struck by the resemblance of the hills and valleys of Camporeno to the holy places of Palestine, began the erection of the "devout chapels" which were to contain the representations of the Passion; and thus arose the group of buildings now forming the monastery of San Vivaldo.

As we drove up we saw several monks at work in the woods and in the vegetable-gardens below the monastery. These took no notice of us, but in answer to our coachman's summons there appeared another, whose Roman profile might have emerged from one of those great portrait-groups of the sixteenth century, where grave-featured monks and chaplains are gathered about a seated pope. This monk, whose courteous welcome betrayed as little surprise as though the lonely glades of San Vivaldo were daily invaded by hordes of sight-seers, informed us that it was his duty to conduct visitors to the various shrines. The chapels of the Passion are about twenty in number, and as many more are said to have perished. They are scattered irregularly through the wood adjoining the monastery, and our guide, who showed a deep interest in the works of art committed to his charge, assured us that the terra-cotta groups were undoubtedly due to Giovanni Gonnelli, *Il Cieco di Gambassi,* for whose talent he seemed to entertain a profound admiration. Some of the master's work, he added, had been destroyed, or replaced by that of "qualche muratore"; but he assured us that in the groups which had been preserved we should at once recognize the touch of an eminent hand. As he led the way he smilingly referred to Giovanni Gonnelli's legendary blindness, which plays a most picturesque part in the artist's biography. The monk explained to us that Gonnelli was blind of only one eye, thus demolishing Baldinucci's charming tradition of portrait-busts executed in total darkness to the amazement of popes and princes. Still, we suspected our guide of adapting his hero's exploits to the incredulity of the unorthodox, and perhaps secretly believing in the anecdotes over which he affected to smile. On the threshold of the first chapel he paused to explain

that some of the groups had been irreparably injured
during the period of neglect and abandonment which
followed the suppression of the monastery. The
government, he added, had seized the opportunity to
carry off from the church the Presepio in high relief
which was Gonnelli's masterpiece, and to strip many
of the chapels of the escutcheons in Robbia ware that
formerly ornamented the ceilings. "Even then,
however," he concluded, "our good fathers were
keeping secret watch over the shrines, and they saved
some of the escutcheons by covering them with whitewash; but the government has never given us back
our Presepio."

Having thus guarded us against possible disillu-
sionment, he unlocked the door of the first chapel on
what he declared to be an undoubted work of the
master—the Descent of the Holy Ghost upon the
Disciples.

This group, like all the others at San Vivaldo, is
set in a little apsidal recess at the farther end of the
chapel. I had expected, at best, an inferior imitation
of the seventeenth-century groups in the more famous Via Crucis of Varallo, but to my surprise I
found myself in the presence of a much finer, and

apparently a much earlier, work. The figures, which
are of life-size, are set in a depressed arch, and fitted
into their allotted space with something of the skill
which the Greek sculptors showed in adapting their
groups to the slope of the pediment. In the centre,
the Virgin kneels on a low column or pedestal, which
raises her partially above the surrounding figures of
the disciples. Her attitude is solemnly prayerful,
with a touch of nun-like severity in the folds of the
wimple and in the gathered plaits of the gown beneath her cloak. Her face, furrowed with lines of
grief and age, is yet irradiated by an inner light;
and her hands, like those of all the figures hitherto
attributed to Gonnelli, are singularly graceful and
expressive. The same air of unction, of what the
French call *recueillement,* distinguishes the face
and attitude of the kneeling disciple on the extreme
left; and the whole group breathes that air of devotional simplicity usually associated with an earlier
and less worldly period of art.

Next to this group, the finest is perhaps that of
"Lo Spasimo," the swoon of the Virgin at the sight
of Christ bearing the cross. It is the smallest of the
groups, being less than life-size, and comprising only

the figure of the Virgin supported by the Marys and by two kneeling angels. There is a trace of primitive stiffness in the attempt to render the prostration of the Virgin, but her face expresses an extremity of speechless anguish which is subtly contrasted with the awed but temperate grief of the woman who bends above her; while the lovely countenances of the attendant angels convey another shade of tender participation: the compassion of those who are in the counsels of the Eternal, and know that

In la sua volontade è nostra pace.

In this group the artist has attained to the completest expression of his characteristic qualities: refined and careful modelling, reticence of emotion, and that "gift of tears" which is the last attribute one would seek in the resonant but superficial art of the seventeenth century.

Among other groups undoubtedly due to the same hand are those of Christ Before Pilate, of the Ascension, and of the Magdalen bathing the feet of Christ. In the group of the Ascension the upper part has been grotesquely restored; but the figures of the Virgin and disciples, who kneel below, are apparently untouched, and on their faces is seen that look of wondering ecstasy, that reflection of the beatific vision, which the artist excelled in representing. In every group of the series his Saint John has this luminous look; and in that of the Ascension it brightens even the shrewd bearded countenances of the older disciples. In the scene of Christ before Pilate the figure of Pilate is especially noteworthy: his delicate incredulous lips seem just framing their immortal interrogation. Our guide pointed out that the Roman lictor in this group, who raises his arm to strike the accused Christ, has had his offending hand knocked off by the zeal of the faithful.

The representation of the Magdalen bathing the feet of Christ is noticeable for the fine assemblage of heads about the supper-table. Those of Christ and of his host are peculiarly expressive; and Saint John's look of tranquil tenderness contrasts almost girlishly with the majestic gravity of the neighbouring faces. The Magdalen herself is less happily executed; there is something actually unpleasant in her ramping four-footed attitude as she crawls toward the Christ, and the figure is probably by another hand. In the group of the Crucifixion, for the most part of inferior workmanship, the figures of the two thieves are finely modelled, and their expression of anguish has been achieved with the same sobriety of means which marks all the artist's effects. The remaining groups in the chapels are without special interest, but under the portico of the church there are three fine figures, possibly by the artist of the Spasimo, representing Saint Roch, Saint Linus of Volterra, and one of the Fathers of the Church.

There are, then, among the groups of San Vivaldo, five which appear to be by the same master, in addition to several scattered figures presumably by his hand; all of which have always been attributed to Giovanni Gonnelli, the blind pupil of Pietro Tacca. The figures in these groups are nearly, if not quite, as large as life; they have all been rudely repainted, and are entirely unglazed, though framed in glazed mouldings of the familiar Robbian style.

Professor Ridolfi's information was confirmed by the local tradition, and there seemed no doubt that the groups of San Vivaldo had always been regarded as the work of Gonnelli, an obscure artist living at a time when the greatest masters produced little to

which posterity has conceded any artistic excellence.
But one glance at the terra-cottas sufficed to show
that they could not have been modelled in mid-seven-
teenth century: neither their merits nor their defects
belonged to that period of art. What had the sculptor of San Vivaldo in common with the pupils of
Giovanni Bologna and Il Fiammingo, that tribe of
skilled craftsmen who peopled every church and palace in Italy with an impersonal flock of Junos and
Virgin Marys, Venuses and Magdalens, distin-
guishable only by their official attributes? The more
closely I studied the groups, the more the conviction
grew that they were the work of an artist trained in
an earlier tradition, and still preserving, under the
stiffening influences of convention, a touch of that
individuality and directness of expression which
mark the prime of Tuscan art. The careful modelling of the hands, the quiet grouping, so free from
effort and agitation, the simple draperies, the devotional expression of the faces, all seemed to point to
the lingering influences of the fifteenth century; not
indeed to the fresh charm of its noon, but to the
refinement, the severity, of its close. The glazed
mouldings enclosing the groups, and the coloured

medallions with which the ceilings of the chapels are decorated, suggested a direct connection with the later school of the Robbias; and as I looked I was haunted by a confused recollection of a Presepio seen at the Bargello, and attributed to Giovanni della Robbia or his school. Could this be the high-relief which had been removed from San Vivaldo?

On returning to Florence I went at once to the Bargello, and found, as I had expected, that the Presepio I had in mind was indeed the one from San Vivaldo. I was surprised by the extraordinary re-semblance of the heads to some of those in the groups ascribed to Gonnelli. I had fancied that the modeller of San Vivaldo might have been inspired by the Pre-sepio of the Bargello; but I was unprepared for the identity of treatment in certain details of hair and drapery, and for the recurrence of the same type of face. The Presepio undoubtedly shows greater deli-cacy of treatment; but this is accounted for by the fact that the figures are much smaller, and only in partial relief, whereas at San Vivaldo they are so much detached from the background that they may be regarded as groups of statuary. Again, the glaze which covers all but the faces of the Presepio has preserved its original beauty of colouring, while the groups of San Vivaldo have been crudely daubed with fresh coats of paint, and even of whitewash; and the effect of the Presepio is farther enhanced by an excessively ornate frame of fruit-garlanded pilasters, as well as by its charming predella with small scenes set between panels of arabesque. Altogether, it is a far more elaborate production than the terra-cottas of San Vivaldo, and some of its most graceful details, such as the dance of angels on the stable-roof, are evidently borrowed from the earlier *répertoire* of the Robbias; but in spite of these incidental archaisms no one can fail to be struck by the likeness of the central figures to certain of the statues at San Vivaldo. The head of Saint Joseph in the Presepio, for instance, with its wrinkled penthouse forehead, and the curled and parted beard, suggests at once that of the disciple seated on the right of Saint John in the house of the Pharisee; the same face, though younger, occurs again in the Pentecostal group, and the kneeling female figure in the Presepio is treated in the same manner as the youngest Mary in the group of the Spasimo: even the long rolled-back tresses, with their shell-like convolutions, are the same.

The discovery of this close resemblance deepened the interest of the problem. It seemed hardly credible that a work of such artistic significance as the Via Crucis of San Vivaldo should not long since have been studied and classified. In Tuscany especially, where every phase of fifteenth-century art, including its prolongation in the succeeding century, has been traced and analyzed with such scrupulous care, it was inconceivable that so interesting an example of an essentially Italian style should have escaped notice. There could be no doubt that the groups belonged to the period in question. Since it was impossible not to reject at once the hypothetical seventeenth-century artist content to imitate with servile accuracy a manner which had already fallen into disfavour, it was necessary to assume that a remarkable example of late *quattro-cento* art had remained undiscovered, within a few hours' journey from Florence, for nearly four hundred years. The only reasonable explanation of this oversight seemed to be that, owing to the seclusion of the monastery of San Vivaldo, the groups had never acquired more than local fame, and that, having possibly been restored in the seventeenth century by Giovanni Gonnelli or one of his pupils, they had been ascribed to him by a generation which, having ceased to value the work of the earlier artist, was profoundly impressed by the miraculous skill of the blind modeller, and eager to connect his name with the artistic treasures of the monastery.

To the infrequent sight-seers of the seventeenth and eighteenth centuries, there would be nothing surprising in such an attribution. The perception of differences in style is a recently-developed faculty, and even if a student of art had penetrated to the wilds of San Vivaldo, he would probably have noticed nothing to arouse a doubt of the local tradition. The movement toward a discrimination of styles, which came in the first half of the nineteenth century, was marked, in the study of Italian art, by a contemptuous indifference toward all but a brief period of that art; and the mere fact that a piece of sculpture was said to have been executed in the seventeenth century would, until very lately, have sufficed to prevent its receiving expert attention. Thus the tradition which ascribed the groups of San Vivaldo to Giovanni Gonnelli resulted in concealing them from modern investigation as effectually as though they had been situated in the centre of an unexplored continent, and in procuring for me the rare sensation of an artistic discovery made in the heart of the most carefully-explored artistic hunting-ground of Europe.

My first care was to seek expert confirmation of my theory; and as a step in this direction I made arrangements to have the groups of San Vivaldo photographed by Signor Alinari of Florence. I was obliged to leave Italy before the photographs could be taken; but on receiving them I sent them at once to Professor Ridolfi, who had listened with some natural incredulity to my description of the terracottas; and his reply shows that I had not overestimated the importance of the discovery.

"No sooner," he writes, "had I seen the photographs than I became convinced of the error of attributing them to Giovanni Gonnelli, called *Il Cieco di Gambassi*. I saw at once that they are not the work of an artist of the seventeenth century, but of one living at the close of the fifteenth or beginning of the sixteenth century; of an artist of the school of the Robbias, who follows their precepts and possesses their style. . . . The figures are most beautifully grouped, and modelled with profound sentiment and not a little *bravura*. They do not appear to me to be all by the same author, for the Christ in the house of the Pharisee seems earlier and purer in style, and more robust in manner; also the swoon of the Madonna, . . . which is executed in a grander style than the other reliefs and seems to belong to the first years of the sixteenth century.

" The fact that these terra-cottas are not glazed does not prove that they are not the work of the Robbia school; for Giovanni della Robbia, for example, sometimes left the flesh of his figures unglazed, painting them with the brush; and this is precisely the case in a Presepio of the National Museum " (this is the Presepio of San Vivaldo), " a work of the Robbias, in which the flesh is left unglazed.

" I therefore declare with absolute certainty that it is a mistake to attribute these beautiful works to Giovanni Gonnelli, and that they are undoubtedly a century earlier in date."

SUB UMBRA LILIORUM

AN IMPRESSION OF PARMA

SUB UMBRA LILIORUM

AN IMPRESSION OF PARMA

PARMA, at first sight, lacks the engaging individuality of some of the smaller Italian
towns.   Of the romantic group of ducal
cities extending from Milan to the Adriatic—Parma,
Modena, Ferrara, Urbino—it is the least easy to hit
off in a few strokes, to sum up in a sentence.   Its
component features, however interesting in themselves, fail to blend in one of those memorable wholes
which take instant hold of the traveller's imagination.   The " sights " of Parma must be sought for;
they remain separate isolated facts, and their quest
is enlivened by few of those happy architectural incidents which give to a drive through Ferrara or Ravenna so fine a flavour of surprise.

The devotee of the fourteenth century, trained by
Ruskin to pass without even saluting any expression
of structural art more recent than the first unfolding

of the pointed style, must restrict his investigations to the Baptistery and the outside of the Cathedral; and even the lax eclectic who nurses a secret weakness for the baroque and rejoices in the last frivolous flowering of the eighteenth century, finds little immediate satisfaction for his tastes. The general aspect of Parma is in fact distinctly inexpressive, and its more important buildings have only the relative merit of suggesting happier examples of the same style. This absence of the superlative is, in many Italian cities, atoned for by the episodical charm of the streets: by glimpses of sculptured windows, pillared courtyards, and cornices projecting a perfect curve against the blue; but the houses of Parma are plain almost to meanness, and though their monotonous succession is broken here and there by a palace-front embroidered with the Farnese lilies, it must be owned that, with rare exceptions, these façades have few palatial qualities but that of size. Perhaps not short of Ravenna could be found another Italian town as destitute of the more obvious graces; and nowhere surely but in Italy could so unpromising an exterior hide such varied treasures. To the lover of Italy—the perennial wooer whom every spring

E.C. Peixotto
PARMA 1901

recalls across the Alps—there is a certain charm in this external dulness. After being steeped in the mediævalism of Siena, Perugia or Pistoja, after breathing at Vicenza, Modena and Bergamo the very air of Goldoni, Rosalba, and the *commedia dell' arte,* it is refreshing to come on a town that holds back and says: "Find me out." Such a challenge puts the psychologist on his mettle and gives to his quest the stimulus of discovery.

It may seem paradoxical to connect the emotions of the explorer with one of the most familiar centres of artistic influence, but it is partly because Parma is still dominated by Correggio that it has dropped out of the emotional range of the modern traveller. For though it is scarce a hundred years since our grandparents posted thither to palpitate over the master, their æsthetic point of view is as remote from ours as their mode of locomotion. By a curious perversity of fate Correggio, so long regarded as the leading exponent of "sentiment," now survives only by virtue of his technique, and has shrunk to the limited immortality of the painter's painter. A new generation may rediscover his emotional charm, but to the untechnical picture-lover of the present day his pro-

digious manipulations of light and colour seldom
atone for the Turveydrop attitudes of his saints and
angels and for the sugary loveliness of his Madonnas.
Lacking alike the frank naturalism of such masters
as Palma Vecchio and Bonifazio, the sensuous mys-
ticism of Sodoma and the fantastic gaiety of Tiepolo,
Correggio seems to typify that phase of cold senti-
mentality which dwindled to its end in the "Keep-
sakes" of sixty years ago. Each generation makes
certain demands on the art of its own period and
seeks certain affinities in the art of the past; and a
kind of personal sincerity is perhaps what modern
taste has most consistently exacted: the term being
understood not in its technical sense, as applied to
execution, but in its imaginative significance, as
qualifying the "message" of the artist. It is inevitable that the average spectator should look at
pictures from a quite untechnical standpoint. He
knows nothing of values, brushwork and the rest; yet
it is to the immense majority formed by his kind
that art addresses itself. There must therefore be
two recognized ways of judging a picture—by its
technique and by its expression: that is, not the mere
story it has to tell, but its power of rendering in line

and colour the equivalent of some idea or of some
emotion. There is the less reason for disputing such
a claim because, given the power of *seeing soul,* as
this faculty may be defined, the power of embodying
the impression, of making it visible and comprehen-
sible to others, is necessarily one of technique; and it
is doubtful if any artist not possessed of this insight
has received, even from his fellow-craftsmen, a lasting award of supremacy.

Now the sentiment that Correggio embodied is
one which, from the present point of view, seems
to lack the preserving essence of sincerity. It is
true that recent taste has returned with a certain passion to the brilliant mannerisms of the eighteenth
century; but it is because they are voluntary mannerisms, as frankly factitious as the masquerading
of children, that they have retained their hold on the
fancy. As there is a soul in the games of children,
or in any diversion entered into with conviction, so
there is a soul, if only an inconsequent spoiled child's
soul, in the laughing art of the eighteenth century.
It is the defect of Correggio's art that it expresses
no conviction whatever. He offers us no clue to the
état d'âme of his celestial gymnasts. They do not

seem to be honestly in love with this world or the next, or to take any personal part in the transactions in which the artist has engaged them. In fact, they are simply models, smirking and attitudinizing at so much an hour, and so well trained that even their individuality as models remains hidden behind the fixed professional smile. The conclusion is that if they are only models to the spectator, it is because they were only models to Correggio; that his art had no transmuting quality, and that he was always conscious of the wires which held on the wings.

It may, indeed, be argued that devotional painting in Italy had assumed, in the sixteenth century, a stereotyped form from which a stronger genius than Correggio's could hardly have freed it; and that the triumphs of that day should be sought rather in the domain of decorative art, where conventionality becomes a strength, and where the æsthetic imagination finds expression in combinations of mere line and colour. Many of the decorative paintings of the sixteenth century are indeed among the most delightful products of Italian art; and it might have been expected that Correggio's extraordinary technical skill and love of rhythmically whirling lines would have found complete development in this direction. It is, of course, permissible to the artist to regard the heavenly hosts as mere factors in a decorative composition; and to consider Thrones, Dominations, Princedoms, Virtues, Powers only in their relation to the diameter of a dome or to the curve of a spandril; but to the untechnical spectator such a feat is almost impossible, and in judging a painter simply as a decorator, the public is more at its ease before such frankly ornamental works as the famous frescoes of the convent of Saint Paul. It might, in fact, have been expected that Correggio would be at his best in executing the commission of the light-hearted Abbess, who had charged him to amplify the symbolism of her device (the crescent moon) by adorning her apartments with the legend of Diana. There is something delightfully characteristic of the period in this choice of the Latmian goddess to typify the spirit of monastic chastity; and equally characteristic is Correggio's acceptance of the commission as an opportunity to paint classic bas-reliefs and rosy flesh and blood, without much attempt to express the somewhat strained symbolism of the myth.

The vaulted ceiling of the room is treated as a

trellised arbour, through which rosy loves peep down on the blonde Diana emerging from grey drifts of evening mist: a charming composition, with much grace of handling in the figure of the goddess and in the *grisailles* of the lunettes below the cornice; yet lacking as a whole just that ethereal quality which is supposed to be the distinctive mark of Correggio's art. Compared with the delicate trellis-work and flitting cupids of Zucchero's frescoes at the Villa di Papa Giulio, Correggio's design is heavy and dull. The masses of foliage are too uniform and the *putti* too fat and stolid for their skyey task. This failure of the decorative sense is rendered more noticeable by the happy manner in which Araldi, a generation earlier, had solved a similar problem in the adjoining room. Here the light arabesques and miniature divinities of the ceiling, and the biblical and mythological scenes of the frieze, are presented with all that earnest striving after personal truth of expression that is the ruling principle of fifteenth-century art. It is this faculty of personal interpretation, always kept in strict abeyance to the laws of decorative fitness, which makes the mural painting of the fifteenth century so satisfying that, compared with

the Mantegna room at Mantua, the Sala del Cambio at Perugia, the Sala degli Angeli at Urbino, and the frescoed room at the Schifanoia at Ferrara, all the later wall-decorations in Italy (save perhaps the Moretto room at Brescia) seem to fall a little short of perfection.

Of a much earlier style of mural painting, Parma itself contains one notable example. The ancient octagon of the Baptistery, with its encircling arcade and strange frieze of leaping, ramping and running animals, is outwardly one of the most interesting buildings in Italy; while its interior has a character of its own hardly to be matched even in that land of fiercely competing individualism. Downward from the apex of the dome the walls are frescoed in successive tiers with figures of saints in rigid staring attitudes, interspersed with awkward presentments of biblical story. All these designs are marked by a peculiar naïveté of composition and great vehemence of gesture and expression. Those in the dome and between the windows are attributed to the thirteenth century, while the lower frescoes are of the fourteenth; but so crude in execution are the latter that they combine with the upper rows in producing an

effect of exceptional decorative value, to which a note
of strangeness is given by the introduction, here and
there, of high-reliefs of saints and angels, so placed
that the frescoes form a background to their projecting figures. The most successful of these sculptures
is the relief of the flight into Egypt: a solemn procession led by a squat square-faced angel with un-
wieldy wings and closed by two inscrutable-looking
figures in Oriental dress.

Seen after the Baptistery, the Cathedral is perhaps something of a disappointment; yet to pass
from its weather-beaten front, between the worn red
lions of the ancient porch, into the dusky magnifi-
cence of the interior, is to enjoy one of those contrasts possible only in a land where the humblest
wayside chapel may disclose the stratified art of centuries. In the great cupola, Correggio lords it with
the maelstrom of his heavenly host; and the walls of
the nave are covered with frescoes by Mazzola and
Gambara, to which time has given a golden-brown
tone, as of sumptuous hangings, that atones for the
pretentious insignificance of their design. There is a
venerable episcopal throne attributed to Benedetto
Antelami, that strangely dramatic sculptor to whom

the reliefs of the Baptistery are also ascribed, and one of the chapels contains a magnificent Descent from the Cross with his signature; but except for these works the details of the interior, though including several fine sepulchral monuments and a ciborium by Alberti, are not exceptional enough to make a lasting impression.

On almost every Italian town, whatever succession of masters it may have known, some one family has left its dominant mark; and Parma is distinctively the city of the Farnesi. Late-comers though they were, their lilies are everywhere, over gateways, on palace-fronts and in the aisles of churches; and they have bequeathed to the town a number of its most characteristic buildings, from the immense unfinished Palazzo della Pilotta to the baroque fountain of parti-coloured marbles which enlivens with its graceful nymphs and river-gods the grassy solitude of the palace-square. It is to Rannuccio I, the greatest of these ducal builders, that Parma owes the gigantic project of the Pilotta, as well as the Farnese theatre and the University. To this group Duke Ottavio, at a later date, added the charming " Little Palace of the Garden," of which the cheerful yellow façade still overlooks the pleached alleys of a formal pleasance adorned, under the Bourbon rulers who succeeded him, with groups of statuary by the court sculptor, a Frenchman named Jean Baptiste Boudard. Ottavio commissioned Agostino Carracci to decorate the interior of the ducal villa, and even now, after years of incredible neglect and ill-usage, the walls of several rooms show remains of the work executed, as the artist's pious inscription runs, *sub umbra liliorum*. The villa has been turned into barracks, and it is difficult to gain admission; but the persistent sight-seer may succeed in seeing one room, where large-limbed ruddy immortals move, against a background of bluish summer landscape, through the slow episodes of some Olympian fable. This apartment shows the skill of the Carracci as decorators of high cool ceremonious rooms, designed to house the midsummer idleness of a court still under the yoke of Spanish etiquette, and living in a climate where the linear vivacities of Tiepolo might have been conducive to apoplexy.

The most noteworthy building which arose in Parma under the shadow of the lilies is, however, the famous theatre built by Aleotti for Duke Rannuccio,

E. C. Peixotto
PARMA · 1901 ·

and opened in 1620 to celebrate the marriage of Odo-
ardo Farnese with Margaret of Tuscany. Externally it is a mere outgrowth of the palace; but to
those who feel a tenderness for the vivacious figures
of the *commedia dell' arte* and have followed their
picturesque wanderings through the pages of Gozzi
and Goldoni, the interior is an immediate evocation
of the strolling theatrical life of the seventeenth
and eighteenth centuries—that strange period when
players were passed on from duchy to principality
to perform at wedding-feasts and to celebrate political victories; when kings and princes stood spon-
sors to their children, and the Church denied them
Christian burial.

The Farnese theatre is one of those brilliant improvisations in wood and plaster to which Italian
artists were trained by centuries of hurriedly-organ-
ized *trionfi,* state processions, religious festivals, re-
turns from war, all demanding the collaboration of
sculptor, architect and painter in the rapid creation
of triumphal arches, architectural perspectives, statuary, chariots, flights of angels, and galleons tossing
on simulated seas: evanescent visions of some *pays
bleu* of Boiardo or of Ariosto, destined to crumble

the next day like the palace of an evil enchanter. To
those who admire the peculiarly Italian gift of spon-
taneous plastic invention, the art of the *plasticatore,*
to borrow an untranslatable term, such buildings are
of peculiar interest, since, owing to the nature of
their construction, so few have survived; and of
these probably none is as well preserved as Aleotti's
theatre. The ceiling of painted canvas is gone, and
the splendid Farnese dukes bestriding their chargers
in lofty niches on each side of the proscenium are
beginning to show their wooden anatomy through
the wounds in their plaster sides; but the fine composition of the auditorium, and the throng of stucco
divinities attitudinizing in the niches and on the bal-
ustrades, and poised above the arch of the proscenium, still serve to recall the original splendour of the
scene. The dusty gloom of the place suggests some
impending transformation, and when fancy has restored to the roof the great glass chandeliers now
hanging in the neighbouring museum, their light
seems to fall once more on boxes draped with crimson
velvet and filled with lords and ladies in the sumptuous Spanish habit, while on the stage, before a gay
perspective of colonnades and terraces, Isabel and

Harlequin and the Capitan Spavento, *plasticatori* of another sort, build on the scaffolding of some familiar intrigue the airy superstructure of their wit.

In the adjoining palace no such revival is possible. Most museums in Italy are dead palaces, and none is more inanimate than that of Parma. Many of the ducal treasures are still left—family portraits by Suttermans and Sir Antony Mor, Bernini-like busts of the Bourbon dukes of Parma, with voluminous wigs and fluttering steinkerks; old furniture, old majolica, and all those frail elaborate trifles that the irony of fate preserves when brick and marble crumble. All these accessories of a ruined splendour, catalogued, numbered and penned up in glass cases, can no more revive the life of which they formed a part than the contents of an herbarium can renew the scent and murmur of a summer meadow. The transient holders of all that pomp, from the great Alexander to the Duchess Marie Louise of Austria, his last unworthy successor, look down with unrecognizing eyes on this dry alignment of classified objects; and one feels, in passing from one room to another, as though some fanciful heroic poem, depicting the splendid vanities of life, and depending

[123]

for its effect on a fortunate collocation of words, had been broken up and sorted out into the different parts of speech.

This is the view of the sentimentalist; but from that of the student of art the museum of Parma is perhaps more interesting than the palace could ever have been. The Correggios are in themselves an unmatched possession; the general collection of pictures is large and varied, and the wealth of bronzes and marbles, of coins, medals and architectural fragments of different schools and periods, would be remarkable in any country but Italy, where the inexhaustible richness of the small towns is a surprise to the most experienced traveller.

On the whole, the impression carried away from Parma is incomplete and confusing. The name calls forth as many scattered images as contradictory associations. It is doubtful if the wanderer reviewing from a distance his Italian memories will be able to put any distinct picture of the place beside the concrete vision of Siena, Mantua or Vicenza. It will not hang as a whole in the gallery of his mental vignettes; but in the mosaic of detached impressions some rich and iridescent fragments will represent his after-thoughts of Parma.

MARCH IN ITALY

MARCH IN ITALY

I

MARCH is in some respects the most exquisite month of the Italian year. It is the month of transitions and surprises, of vehement circling showers with a golden heart of sunlight, of bare fields suffused overnight with fruit-blossoms, and hedgerows budding as suddenly as the staff of Tannhäuser. It is the month in which the northern traveller, grown distrustful of the promised clemency of Italian skies, and with the winter bitterness still in his bones, lighting on a patch of primroses under a leafless bank, or on the running flame of tulips along the trenches of an olive orchard, learns that Italy *is* Italy, after all, and hugs himself at thought of the black ultramontane March.

It must be owned, however, that it is not, even in Italy, the safest month for excursions. There are too many *voltes-face* toward winter, too many moody hesitating dawns, when the skies will not declare themselves for or against rain, but hanging neutral till the hesitating traveller sets forth, seem then to take a cruel joy in proving that he should have stayed at home.   Yet there are rare years when some benign influence tames the fitfulness of March, subduing her to a long sequence of golden days, and then he who has trusted to her promise receives the most exquisite reward.   It takes faith in one's luck to catch step with such a train of days, and fare with them northward across the wakening land; but now and then this fortune befalls the pilgrim, and then he sees a new Italy, an Italy which discovery seems to make his own.   The ancient Latin landscape, so time-furrowed and passion-scarred, lies virgin to the eye, fresh-bathed in floods of limpid air.   The scene seems recreated by the imagination, it wears the pristine sparkle of those

Towers of fables immortal fashioned from mortal dreams

which lie beyond the geographer's boundaries, like the Oceanus of the early charts; it becomes, in short, the land in which anything may happen, save the dull, the obvious and the expected.

II

IT was, for instance, on such a March day that we rowed across the harbour of Syracuse to the mouth of the Anapus.

Our brown rowers, leaping overboard, pushed the flat-bottomed boat through the line of foam where bay and river meet, and we passed over to the smooth current which slips seaward between flat banks fringed with arundo donax and bamboo. The bamboo grows in vast feathery thickets along these Sicilian waters, and the slightly angular precision of its stem and foliage allies itself well with the classic clearness of the landscape—a landscape which, in spite of an occasional excess of semi-tropical vegetation, yet retains the Greek quality of producing intense effects with a minimum of material. There is nothing tropical about the shores of the Anapus; but as the river turns and narrows, the boat passes under an arch of Egyptian papyrus, that slender exotic reed, brought to Sicily, it is supposed, by her Arabian colonizers, and thriving, strangely enough, in no other European soil. This plumy tunnel so enclosed us as we advanced, that for long stretches of our indolent progress we saw only the face of the stream, the summer insects flickering on it, and the continuous golden line of irises along its edge. Now and then, however, a gap in the papyrus showed, as through an arch in a wall, a prospect of flat fields with grazing cattle, or a solitary farm-house, low, brown, *tassée,* with a date-palm spindling against its well-curb, or the white flank of Etna suddenly thrust across the sky-line.

So, after a long dreamy lapse of time, we came to the source of the river, the azure bowl of the nymph Cyane, who pours her pure current into the broader Anapus. The haunt of the nymph is a circular reed-fringed pool, supposedly so crystalline that she may still be seen lurking on its pebbly bed; but the recent spring rains had clouded her lair, and though, in this legend-haunted land, one always feels the nearness of

The faun pursuing, the nymph pursued,

the pool of Cyane revealed no sign of her presence.

Disappointed in our quest, we turned back and glided down the Anapus again to visit her sister-nymph, the more famed but less fortunate Arethusa, whose unhappy fate it is to mingle her wave with the brackish sea-tide in the very harbour of Syracuse, where, under the wall of the quay, the poor creature languishes in a prison of masonry, her papyrus wreath sending up an anæmic growth from the slimy bottom filled with green.

We were glad to turn from this desecrated fount to the long russet-coloured town curving above its harbour. Syracuse, girt with slopes of flowering orchard-land, lies nobly against the fortified ridge of Epipolæ. But the city itself—richer in history than any other on that crowded soil, and characteristically symbolized by its Greek temple welded into the masonry of a mediæval church—even the thronging associations of the city could not, on a day so prodigal of sunlight, hold us long within its walls. These walls, the boundaries of the Greek Ortygia, have once more become the limits of the shrunken modern town, and crossing the moat beyond them, we found ourselves at once in full country. There was a peculiar charm in the sudden transition from the old brown streets saturated with history to this clear smiling land where only the spring seemed to have written its tale—its ever-recurring, ever-fresh record of blossom and blade miraculously renewed. The country about

Syracuse is peculiarly fitted to be the exponent of this gospel of renewal. The land stretches away in mild slopes laden with acre on acre of blossoming fruit-trees, and of old olive orchards under which the lilac anemones have room to spread in never-ending sheets of colour. The open pastures are plumed with silvery asphodel, and every farm-house has its glossy orange-grove fenced from the road by a rampart of prickly pear.

The highway itself, as we drove out toward Epipolæ, was thronged with country-folk who might have been the descendants of Theocritan nymphs and mortal shepherds, brown folk with sidelong agate eyes, trudging dustily after their goats and asses, or jogging townward in their little blue or red carts painted with legends of the saints and stories from Ariosto. After a mile or two the road curved slowly upward and we began to command a widening prospect. At our feet lay Syracuse, girt by the Plemmyrian marsh, and by the fields and orchards which were once the crowded Greek suburbs of Neapolis, Tyche and Achradina; and beyond the ridge of Epipolæ and the nearer hills, Etna rose white and dominant against the pale Calabrian coast-line.

The fortress of Euryalus, on the crest of Epipolæ, might be called the Greek Carcassonne, since it is the best-preserved example of ancient military architecture in Europe. Archways, galleries, massive flights of stairs and long subterranean passages may still be traced by the archæologically minded in the mass of fallen stones marking the site of the ruin; and even the idler unversed in military construction will feel the sudden nearness of the past when he comes upon the rock-hewn sockets to which the cavalry attached their horses.

Euryalus, however, more fortunate than Carcassonne, has escaped the renovating hand of a Viollet-le-Duc, and its broken ramparts lie in mellow ruin along the backbone of the ridge, feathered with those delicate growths which, in the Mediterranean countries, veil the fallen works of man without concealing them. That day, indeed, the prodigal blossoming of the Sicilian March had covered the ground with a suffusion of colour which made even the mighty ruins of the fortress seem a mere background for the triumphant pageant of the spring. From the tall silhouette of the asphodel, classic in outline as in name, to the tendrils of scarlet and yellow vetch capriciously fretting the ancient stones with threads of richest colour, every inch of ground and every cleft of masonry was overrun with some delicate wild tracery of leaf and blossom.

But to those who first see Syracuse in the month of March—the heart of the Sicilian spring—it must appear pre-eminently as one vast unbounded garden. The appeal of architecture and history pales before this vast glory of the loosened soil. The walls and towers will remain—but this transient beauty must be caught upon the wing. And so from the flowered slopes of Euryalus we passed to the richer profusion of the gardens that adjoin the town. Fringing the road by which we descended, a hundred spring flowers—anemones, lupins, sweet alyssum, herb-Robert, snapdragon and the fragrant wild mignonette—linked the uncultivated country-side to the rich horticulture of the suburbs; and in the suburbs the vegetation reached so tropical an excess that the spring pilgrim's memory of Syracuse must be a blur of golden-brown ruins immersed in a sea of flowers.

There are gardens everywhere, gardens of all kinds and classes, from the peasant's hut hedged with pink geraniums to the villa with its terraced sub-tropical growths; but most wonderful, most unexpected of all, are the famous gardens of the quarries. Time has perhaps never done a more poetic thing than in turning these bare unshaded pits of death, where the Greek captives of Salamis died under the lash of the Sicilian slave-driver and the arrows of the Sicilian sun, into deep cool wells of shade and verdure. Here, where the chivalry of Athens perished of heat and thirst, a damp mantle of foliage pours over the red cliff-sides, fills the depths with the green freshness of twilight, and effaces, like a pitiful hand on a burning brow, the record of that fiery martyrdom. And the quarries are as good to grow flowers in as to torture men. The equable warmth of these sheltered ravines is as propitious to vegetation as it was destructive to human life; and wherever soil has accumulated, on the ledges and in the hollows, the "blood of the martyrs" sends up an exuberant growth.

On the edge of one of these hell-pits a monastery has been built; above another stands a villa; and monastic and secular hands have transformed the sides of the quarries into gardens of fantastic beauty. Paths and rocky stairways fringed with fern wind down steeply from the upper world, now tunnelled through dense growths of cypress and olive, now skirting cliff-walks dripping with cataracts of ivy, or tufted with the glaucous spikes and scarlet rockets of gigantic cactuses. In the depths, where time has amassed a soil incredibly rich, the vegetation becomes prodigious, febrile, like that of the delirious garden in "La Faute de l'Abbé Mouret." Here the paths wind under groves of orange and lemon trees, over a dense carpeting of violets, stocks, narcissus and honey-scented hyacinths. Trellises of red roses lift their network against the light, and damp clefts of the rock are black with dripping maidenhair. Here are tall hedges of blue rosemary and red-gold abutilon, there shrubby masses of anthemisia, heliotrope and lavender. Overhead, black cypress-shafts spring from the bright sea of foliage, and at the pit's brink, where the Syracusan citizens, under their white umbrellas, used to lean over and taunt the captives dying in the sun, a great hedge of prickly pear writhes mockingly against the sky.

III

At noon of such another day we set out from Rome
for Caprarola.

The still air had a pearly quality and a mauve haze
hung upon the hills. Our way lay north-westward,
toward the Ciminian mountains. Once free of the
gates, our motor started on its steady rush along the
white highway, first past the walls of vineyard and
garden, and then across the grey waste spaces of the
Campagna. The Roman champaign is the type of
variety in monotony. Seen from the heights of the
city, it reaches in silvery sameness toward all points
of the compass; but to a near view it reveals a dozen
different physiognomies. Toward Frascati and the
Alban hills it wears the ordered garb of fertility:
wheat-fields, vineyards and olive-groves. South-
eastward, in the direction of the Sabine range, its
white volcanic reaches are tufted with a dark *maqui*
of sullen and reluctant growth, while in the west the
Agro Romano rolls toward Monterosi and Soracte
in sere reaches of pasture-land mottled with hillock
and ravine.

Gradually, as we left the outskirts of Rome, the

grandeur of this stern landscape declared itself. To the right and left the land stretched out in endless grassy reaches, guarded here and there by a lonely tomb or by the tall gateway of some abandoned vineyard. Presently the road began to rise and dip, giving us, on the ascent, sweeping views over a wider range of downs which rolled away in the north-west to the Ciminian forest, and in the east to the hazy rampart of the Sabine hills. Ahead of us the same undulations swept on interminably, the road undulating with them, now engulfed in the trough of the land, now tossed into view on some farther slope, like a streak of light on a flying sea. There was something strangely inspiriting in the call of this fugitive road. From ever-lengthening distances it seemed to signal us on, luring us up slope after slope, and racing ahead of us down the long declivities where the motor panted after it like a pack on the trail.

For some time the thrill of the chase distracted us from a nearer view of the foreground; but gradually there stole on us a sense of breadth and quietude, of sun-bathed rugged fields with black cattle grazing in their hollows, and here and there a fortified farmhouse lifting its bulk against the sky. These fortress-farms of the Campagna, standing sullen and apart among the pacific ruins of pagan Rome— tombs, aqueducts and villas—give a glimpse of that black age which rose on the wreck of the Imperial civilization. All the violence and savagery of the mediæval city, with its great nobles forever in revolt, its popes plotting and trembling within the Lateran walls, or dragging their captive cardinals from point to point as the Emperor or the French King moved his forces—all the mysterious crimes of passion and cupidity, the intrigues, ambushes, massacres with which the pages of the old chronicles reek, seem symbolized in one of those lowering brown piles with its battlemented sky-line, crouched on a knoll of the waste land which its masters helped to devastate.

At length a blue pool, the little lake of Monterosi, broke the expanse of the downs; then we flashed through a poor roadside village of the same name, and so upward into a hill-region where hedgerows and copses began to replace the brown tufting of the Campagna. On and on we fled, ever upward to the town of Ronciglione, perched, like many hill-cities of this region, on the sheer edge of a ravine, and stretching its line of baroque churches and stately crumbling palaces along one steep street to the edge of a lofty down.

Across this plateau, golden with budding broom, we flew on to the next height, and here paused to embrace the spectacle—beneath us, on the left, the blue volcanic lake of Vico in its oak-fringed crater; on the right, far below, the plain of Etruria, scattered with ancient cities and ringed in a mountain-range still touched with snow; and rising from the middle of the plain, Soracte, proud, wrinkled, solitary, with the ruined monastery of Sant' Oreste just seen on its crest.

From this mount of vision we dropped abruptly downward by a road cut in the red tufa-banks. Presently there began to run along the crest of the tufa on our left a lofty wall gripping the flanks of the rock, and overhung by dark splashes of ivy and clumps of leafless trees—one of those rugged Italian walls which are the custodians of such hidden treasures of scent and verdure. This wall continued to run parallel with us till our steep descent ended in a stone-paved square, with the roofs of a town sliding abruptly away below it on one side, and above, on the other, the great ramps and terraces

of a pentagonal palace clenched to the highest ledge of the cliff. Such is the first sight of Caprarola.

Never, surely, did feudal construction so insolently dominate its possessions. The palace of the great Farnese Cardinal seems to lord it not only over the golden-brown town which forms its footstool, but over the far-reaching Etrurian plain, the forests and mountains of the horizon: over Nepi, Sutri, Cività Castellana, and the lonely pride of Soracte. And the grandeur of the site is matched by the arrogance of the building: no villa, but a fortified and moated palace, or rather a fortress planned in accordance with the most advanced military science of the day, but built on the lines of a palace. Yet on such a March day as this, with the foreground of brown oak-woods all slashed and fringed with rosy almond-bloom; with the haze of spring just melting from the horizon, and revealing depth after depth of mountain-blue; with March clouds fleeing overhead, and flinging trails of shadow and showers of silver light across the undulations of the plain—on such a day, the insolent Farnese keep, for all its background of gardens, frescoes, and architectural splendour, seems no longer

the lord of the landscape, but a mere point of vantage
from which to view the outspread glory at our feet.

IV

THE drive from Viterbo to Montefiascone lies across
the high plateau between the Monte Cimino and the
lake of Bolsena.

For the best part of the way, the landscape is pastoral and agricultural, with patches of oak-wood to
which in March the leaves still cling; and on this fit-
ful March morning, with rain in the shifting clouds,
the ploughmen move behind their white oxen under
umbrellas as vividly green as the young wheat. Here
are none of the great bursts of splendour which mark
the way from Rome to Caprarola; and it seems fitting that this more prosaic road should be travelled
at a sober pace, in a Viterban posting-chaise, behind
two plodding horses. The horses are not so plodding, however, but that they swing us briskly enough
down the short descents of the rolling country, which
now becomes wilder and more diversified, with
stretches of woodland interspersed with a heathy
growth of low fragrant shrubs. Here the slopes are

thick with primroses, and the blue vinca and violet peep through the ivy trails of the hedgerows; but the trees are still leafless, for it is a high wind-swept region, where March practises few of her milder arts. A lonely country too: no villages, and only a few solitary farm-houses, are to be seen as we jog up and down the monotonous undulations of the road to the foot of Montefiascone.

The town overhangs us splendidly, on a spur above the lake of Bolsena; and a long ascent between fortified walls leads to the summit on which its buildings are huddled. Through the curtain of rain which the skies have now let down, the crooked streets with their archways and old blackened stone houses present no striking effects, though doubtless a bright day would draw from them some of that latent picturesqueness which is never far to seek when Italian masonry and Italian sunlight meet. Meanwhile, however, the rain persists, and the environment of Montefiascone remains so obstinately shrouded that, for all we know, the town may be situated "Nowhere," like the famous scene in Festus.

Through this rain-muffled air, led blindfold as it were, we presently descend again by the same wind-

ings to the city gates, and thence, following the road
to Bagnorea, come on the desolate church of San
Flaviano, lying by itself in a hollow beneath the walls
of the town.   In our hasty dash from the carriage to
the door, there is just time to receive the impression
of an immensely old brick façade, distorted and
scarred with that kind of age which only the Latin
sense of antiquity has kept a word to describe—then
we are in a low-arched cavernous interior, with spec-
tral frescoes emerging here and there from the uni-
versal background of whitewash, and above the choir
a spreading gallery or upper church, which makes of
the lower building a species of crypt above ground.
And here—O irony of fate!—in this old, deserted
and damp-dripping church, under a worn slab before
the abandoned altar (for it is only in the upper
church that mass continues to be said) —here, a casta-
way as it were from both worlds, lies that genial off-
shoot of a famous race, the wine-loving Bishop Fug-
ger, whose lust of the palate brought him to this
lonely end.   It would have been impossible to pass
through Montefiascone without dropping a com-
memorative tear on the classic Est-Est-Est upon
which, till so lately, a good cask of Montefiascone has

been yearly broached in memory of the prelate's end; yet one feels a regret, almost, in carrying away such a chill recollection of the poor Bishop's fate, in leaving him to the solitude of that icy limbo which seems so disproportionate a punishment for his amiable failing.

Leaving San Flaviano, we press on toward Orvieto through an unbroken blur of rain. The weary miles leave no trace in memory, and we are still in an indeterminate region of wood and pasture and mist-muffled hills when gradually the downpour ceases, and streaks of sunset begin to part the clouds. Almost at the same moment a dip of the road brings us out above a long descent, with a wavy plain at its base, and reared up on a cliff above the plain a fierce brown city, walled, towered and pinnacled, which seems to have dropped from the sky like some huge beast of prey and locked its talons in the rock. All about the plain, in the watery evening light, rises a line of hills, with Monte Amiata thrusting its peak above the circle; the nearer slopes are clothed in olive and cypress, with castles and monasteries jutting from their ledges, and just below us the sight of an arched bridge across a ravine, with a clump of trees at its approach, touches a spring of memory and transports us from the actual scene to its pictured presentment—Turner's "Road to Orvieto."

It was, in fact, from this point that the picture was painted; and looking forth on the landscape, with its stormy blending of sepia-hues washed in pallid sunlight, one sees in it the vindication of Turner's art —that true impressionism which consists not in the unimaginative noting of actual "bits," but in the reconstruction of a scene as it has flowed into the mould of memory, the merging of fragmentary facts into a homogeneous impression. This is what Turner has done to the view of Orvieto from the Bolsena road, so summing up and interpreting the spirit of the scene that the traveller pausing by the arched bridge above the valley loses sense of the boundaries between art and life, and lives for a moment in that mystical region where the two are one.

V

OUR friends and counsellors had for many years warned us against visiting Vallombrosa in March— the month which oftenest finds us in Tuscany.

"Wait till June," they advised—and knowing the complexity of influences which go to make up an Italian "sensation," and how, for lack of one ingredient, the whole mixture may lose its savour, we had obediently waited for June. But June in Florence never seemed to come—"the time and the place" were no more to meet in our horoscope than in the poet's; and so, one year when March was playing at April, we decided to take advantage of her mood and risk the adventure.

We set out early, in that burnished morning air which seems, as with a fine burin, to retrace overnight every line of the Tuscan landscape. The railway runs southward along the Arno valley to Sant' Ellero; and we might have been travelling through some delicately-etched background of Mantegna's or Robetta's, in which the clear pale colours of early spring were but an effect of subtle blendings of line. This Tuscan hill scenery, which for purity of modelling has no match short of Greece, is seen to the best advantage in March, when the conformation of the land is still unveiled by foliage, and every line tells like the threads of silver in a *niello*.

From Sant' Ellero, where the train is exchanged

for a little funicular car of primitive construction, we were pushed jerkily uphill by a gasping engine which had to be constantly refreshed by long draughts of water from wayside tanks. On such a day, however, it was impossible to grudge the slowness of the ascent. As we mounted higher, the country developed beneath us with that far-reaching precision of detail which gives to extended views in mid-Italy a curiously pre-Raphaelite look—as though they had been wrought out by a hand enamoured of definition and unskilled in the creation of general effects. The new wheat springing under the olives was the only high note of colour: all else was sepia-brown of new-turned earth, grey-brown of weather-mottled farm-houses and village belfries, golden-black of rusty cypresses climbing the hill-sides in straight interminable lines, and faint blush of peach-blossoms floating against grey olives.

Then we gained a new height, and the details of the foreground were lost in a vast unfolding of distances—hill on hill, blurred with olive-groves, or bare and keen-cut, with a sprinkling of farm-houses on their slopes, and here and there a watch-tower on a jutting spur; and beyond these again, a tossing sunlit sea of peaks, its farthest waves still crested with snow. Half way up, the abrupt slopes of oak-forest which we had skirted gave way to a plateau clothed with vines and budding fruit orchards; then another sharp climb through oak-scrub, across the dry beds of mountain-streams and up slopes of broom and heather, brought us to the topmost ledge, where the railway ends. On this ledge stands the dreary village of Saltina—a cluster of raw-looking houses set like boxes on a shelf (with a Hôtel Milton among them), and a background of Swiss chalets dotted forlornly on a treeless slope. Saltina must be arid even in midsummer, and in March it was a place to fly from. Our flight, however, was regulated by the leisurely gait of a small white donkey who was the only *bête de somme* to be had at that early season, and behind whom we slowly turned the shoulder of the cliff, and entered the pillared twilight of a great fir-wood. The road ran through this wood for a mile or two, carrying us straight to the heart of the Etrurian shades. As we advanced, byways branched off to the right and left, climbing the hill-sides through deep-perspectives of verdure; and presently we came to a wide turfy hollow, where the great trees recede, leaving a space for the monastery and its adjacent buildings.

The principal *corps-de-bâtiment* faces on a walled entrance-court with box-bordered paths leading to the fine arcaded portico of the church. These buildings are backed by a hanging wood with a hermitage on its crest—the Paradiso—but before them lies an open expanse studded with ancient trees, with a stone-bordered fish-pond, and grass walks leading down to mossy glens with the sound of streams in their depths. Facing the monastery stands the low building where pilgrims were formerly lodged, and which now, without farther modification than the change of name, has become the Albergo della Foresta; while the monastery itself has been turned into a government school of forestry.

Since change was inevitable, it is a fortunate accident which has housed a sylvan college in these venerable shades, and sent the green-accoutred foresters to carry on the husbandry of the monks. Never, surely, were the inevitable modifications of time more gently tempered to the survivor of earlier conditions. The monastery of Vallombrosa has neither the examinate air of a *monument historique,* nor that look

of desecration and decadency that too often comes
with altered uses. It has preserved its high atmosphere of meditative peace, and the bands of students
flitting through the forest with surveying-imple-
ments and agricultural tools seem the lawful suc-
cessors of the monks.

We had been told in Florence that winter still held
the mountains, that we should find snow in the shady
hollows and a glacial wind from the peaks. But
spring airs followed us to the heights. Through the
aromatic fir-boughs the sunlight slanted as warmly
as down the ilex-walks of the Boboli gardens, and
over the open slopes about the monastery there ran a
rosy-purple flush of crocuses—not here and there in
scattered drifts, or starring the grass as in the fore-
grounds of Mantegna and Botticelli, but so close-set
that they formed a continuous sheet of colour, a tide
of lilac which submerged the turf and, flowing between the ancient tree-boles, invaded even the dark
edges of the forest. It was probably the one moment
of the year at which the forest flushes into colour; its
hour of transfiguration—we might have tried every
other season, and missed the miracle of March in Vallombrosa. At first the eye was dazzled by this vast

field of the cloth-of-purple, and could take in none of the more delicate indications of spring; but presently we found our way to the lower glens, where the crocuses ceased, and pale-yellow primroses poured over ivy-banks to the brink of agate-coloured brooks. In the forest, too, ferns were uncurling and violets thrusting themselves through the close matting of fir-needles; while the terraces of the monks' garden, which climbs the hill-side near the monastery, were fragrant with budding box and beds of tulip and narcissus.

It was an air to idle in, breathing deep the stored warmth of immemorial springs; but the little donkey waited between the shafts of his *calessina,* and on the ledge of Saltina we knew that our engine was taking a last draught before the descent. Reluctantly we jogged back through the forest, and, regaining our seats in the train, plunged downward into a sea of translucent mountains, and valleys bathed in haze, a great reach of irradiated heights flowing by imperceptible gradations into amber depths of air, while below us the shadows fell, and the Arno gleamed white in the indistinctness of evening.

PICTURESQUE MILAN

PICTURESQUE MILAN

I

IT is hard to say whether the stock phrase of the stock tourist—" there is so little to see in Milan " —redounds most to the derision of the speaker or to the glory of Italy. That such a judgment should be possible, even to the least instructed traveller, implies a surfeit of impressions procurable in no other land; since, to the hastiest observation, Milan could hardly seem lacking in interest when compared to any but Italian cities. From comparison with the latter, even, it suffers only on a superficial estimate, for it is rich in all that makes the indigenous beauty of Italy, as opposed to the pseudo-Gothicisms, the trans-Alpine points and pinnacles, which Ruskin taught a submissive generation of art critics to regard as the typical expression of the Italian spirit. The guide-books, long accustomed to draw their Liebig's extract

of art from the pages of this school of critics, have
kept the tradition alive by dwelling only on the monuments which conform to perpendicular ideals, and by
apologetic allusions to the "monotony" and "regu-
larity" of Milan—as though endeavouring in advance to placate the traveller for its not looking like
Florence or Siena!

Of late, indeed, a new school of writers, among
whom Mr. J. W. Anderson, and the German authors,
Messrs. Ebe and Gurlitt, deserve the first mention,
have broken through this conspiracy of silence, and
called attention to the intrinsically Italian art of the
post-Renaissance period; the period which, from Michael Angelo to Juvara, has been marked in sculpture and architecture (though more rarely in painting) by a series of memorable names. Signor
Franchetti's admirable monograph on Bernini, and
the recent volume on Tiepolo in the Knackfuss series
of Künstler-Monographien have done their part in
this redistribution of values; and it is now possible
for the traveller to survey the course of Italian art
with the impartiality needful for its due enjoyment,
and to admire, for instance, the tower of the Mangia
without scorning the palace of the Consulta.

II

But, it may be asked, though Milan will seem more interesting to the emancipated judgment, will it appear more picturesque? Picturesqueness is, after all, what the Italian pilgrim chiefly seeks; and the current notion of the picturesque is a purely Germanic one, connoting Gothic steeples, pepper-pot turrets, and the huddled steepness of the northern burgh.

Italy offers little, and Milan least of all, to satisfy these requirements. The Latin ideal demanded space, order, and nobility of composition. But does it follow that picturesqueness is incompatible with these? Take up one of Piranesi's etchings—those strange compositions in which he sought to seize the spirit of a city or a quarter by a mingling of its most characteristic features. Even the northern conception of the picturesque must be satisfied by the sombre wildness of these studies—here a ruined aqueduct, casting its shade across a lonely stretch of ground tufted with acanthus, there a palace colonnade through which the moonlight sweeps on a winter wind, or the recesses of some mighty Roman bath where cloaked figures are huddled in dark confabulation.

Canaletto's black-and-white studies give, in a lesser degree, the same impression of the grotesque and the fantastic—the under-side of that *barocchismo* so long regarded as the smirk on the face of a conventional age.

But there is another, a more typically Italian picturesqueness, gay rather than sinister in its suggestions, made up of lights rather than of shadows, of colour rather than of outline, and this is the picturesqueness of Milan. The city abounds in vivid effects, in suggestive juxtapositions of different centuries and styles—in all those incidental contrasts and surprises which linger in the mind after the catalogued "sights" have faded. Leaving behind the wide modern streets—which have the merit of having been modernized under Eugène Beauharnais rather than under King Humbert—one enters at once upon some narrow byway overhung by the grated windows of a seventeenth-century palace, or by the delicate terra-cotta apse of a *cinque-cento* church. Everywhere the forms of expression are purely Italian, with the smallest possible admixture of that

Gothic element which marks the old free cities of Central Italy. The rocca Sforzesca (the old Sforza castle) and the houses about the Piazza de' Mercanti are the chief secular buildings recalling the pointed architecture of the north; and the older churches are so old that they antedate Gothic influences, and lead one back to the round-arched basilican type. But in the line of national descent what exquisite varieties the Milanese streets present! Here, for instance, is the Corinthian colonnade of San Lorenzo, the only considerable fragment of ancient Mediolanum, its last shaft abutting on a Gothic archway against which clings a flower-decked shrine. Close by, one comes on the ancient octagonal church of San Lorenzo, while a few minutes' drive leads to where the Borromeo palace looks across a quiet grassy square at the rococo front of the old family church, flanked by a fine bronze statue of the great saint and cardinal.

The Palazzo Borromeo is itself a notable factor in the picturesqueness of Milan. The entrance leads to a court-yard enclosed in an ogive arcade surmounted by pointed windows in terra-cotta mouldings. The walls of this court are still frescoed with the Borromean crown, and the *Humilitas* of the haughty race;

and a doorway leads into the muniment-room, where the archives of the house are still stored, and where, on the damp stone walls, Michelino da Milano has depicted the scenes of a fifteenth-century villeggiatura. Here the noble ladies of the house, in high fluted turbans and fantastic fur-trimmed gowns, may be seen treading the measures of a mediæval dance with young gallants in parti-coloured hose, or playing at various games—the *jeu de tarots,* and a kind of cricket played with a long wooden bat; while in the background rise the mountains about Lake Maggiore and the peaked outline of the Isola Bella, then a bare rock unadorned with gardens and architecture. These frescoes, the only existing works of a little-known Lombard artist, are suggestive in style of Pisanello's dry and vigorous manner, and as records of the private life of the Italian nobility in the fifteenth century they are second only to the remarkable pictures of the Schifanoia at Ferrara.

Not far from the Borromean palace, another doorway leads to a different scene: the great cloister of the Ospedale Maggiore, one of the most glorious monuments that man ever erected to his fellows.

The old hospitals of Italy were famous not only for
their architectural beauty and great extent, but for
their cleanliness and order and the enlightened care
which their inmates received. Northern travellers
have recorded their wondering admiration of these
lazarets, which seemed as stately as palaces in comparison with the miserable pest-houses north of the
Alps. What must have been the astonishment of
such a traveller, whether German or English, on setting foot in the principal court of the Milanese hospital, enclosed in its vast cloister enriched with
traceries and medallions of terra-cotta, and surmounted by the arches of an open loggia whence the
patients could look down on a peaceful expanse of
grass and flowers! Even now, one wonders whether
this poetizing of philanthropy, this clothing of char-
ity in the garb of beauty, may not have had its heal-
ing uses: whether the ugliness of the modern hospital
may not make it, in another sense, as unhygienic as
the more picturesque buildings it has superseded? It
is at least pleasant to think of the poor sick people
sunning themselves in the beautiful loggia of the
Ospedale Maggiore, or sitting under the magnolia-
trees in the garden, while their blue-gowned and

black-veiled nurses move quietly through the cloisters at the summons of the chapel-bell.

But one need not enter a court-yard or cross a threshold to appreciate the variety and colour of Milan. The streets themselves are full of charming detail—*quattro-cento* marble portals set with medallions of bushy-headed Sforzas in round caps and plaited tunics; windows framed in terra-cotta wreaths of fruit and flowers; iron balconies etching their elaborate arabesques against the stucco house-fronts; mighty doorways flanked by Atlantides, like that of Pompeo Leoni's house (the *Casa degli Omenoni*) and of the Jesuit seminary; or yellow-brown rococo churches with pyramids, broken pediments, flying angels, and vases filled with wrought-iron palm-branches. It is in summer that these streets are at their best. Then the old gardens overhanging the Naviglio—the canal which intersects Milan with a layer of Venice—repeat in its waters their marble loggias hung with the vine, and their untrained profusion of roses and camellias. Then, in the more aristocratic streets, the palace doorways yield vistas of double and triple court-yards, with creeper-clad arcades enclosing spaces of

shady turf, and terminating perhaps in a fountain set in some splendid architectural composition against the inner wall of the building. In summer, too, the dark archways in the humbler quarters of the town are brightened by fruit-stalls embowered in foliage, and heaped with such melons, figs and peaches as would have driven to fresh extravagance the exuberant brush of a Flemish fruit-painter. Then again, at the turn of a street, one comes across some little church just celebrating the feast of its patron saint with a brave display of garlands and red hangings; while close by a cavernous *bottegha* has been festooned with more garlands and with bright nosegays, amid which hang the painted candles and other votive offerings designed to attract the small coin of the faithful.

III

YET Milan is not dependent on the seasons for this midsummer magic of light and colour. For dark days it keeps its store of warmth and brightness hidden behind palace walls and in the cold dusk of church and cloister. Summer in all its throbbing heat has been imprisoned by Tiepolo in the great ceiling of the Palazzo Clerici: that revel of gods and demigods, and mortals of all lands and races, who advance with linked hands out of the rosy vapours of dawn. Nor are loftier colour-harmonies wanting. On the walls of San Maurizio Maggiore, Luini's virgin martyrs move as in the very afterglow of legend: that hesitating light in which the fantastic becomes probable, and the boundaries between reality and vision fade; while tints of another sort, but as tender, as harmonious, float through the dusk of the sacristy of Santa Maria delle Grazie, a dim room panelled with intarsia-work, with its grated windows veiled by vine-leaves.

But nothing in Milan approaches in beauty the colour-scheme of the Portinari chapel behind the choir of Sant' Eustorgio. In Italy, even, there is nothing else exactly comparable to this masterpiece of collaboration between architect and painter. At Ravenna, the tomb of Galla Placidia and the apse of San Vitale glow with richer hues, and the lower church of Assisi is unmatched in its shifting mystery of chiar'-oscuro; but for pure light, for a clear shadowless scale of iridescent tints, what can approach the

Portinari chapel? Its most striking feature is the harmony of form and colour which makes the decorative design of Michelozzo flow into and seem a part of the exquisite frescoes of Vincenzo Foppa. This harmony is not the result of any voluntary feint, any such trickery of the brush as the later decorative painters delighted in. In the Portinari chapel, architecture and painting are kept distinct in treatment, and the fusion between them is effected by unity of line and colour, and still more, perhaps, by an identity of sentiment, which keeps the whole chapel in the same mood of blitheness,—a mood which makes it difficult to remember that the chapel is the mausoleum of a martyred saint. But Saint Peter Martyr's marble sarcophagus, rich and splendid as it is, somehow fails to distract the attention from its setting. There are so many mediæval monuments like it in Italy—and there is but one Portinari chapel. From the cupola, with its scales of pale red and blue, overlapping each other like the breast-plumage of a pigeon, and terminating in a terra-cotta frieze of dancing angels, who swing between them great bells of fruit and flowers, the eye is led by insensible gradations of tint to Foppa's frescoes in the spandrils—

iridescent saints and angels in a setting of pale classical architecture—and thence to another frieze of
terra-cotta seraphs with rosy-red wings against a
background of turquoise-green; this lower frieze
resting in turn on pilasters of pale green adorned
with white stucco *rilievi* of little bell-ringing angels.
It is only as a part of this colour-scheme that the central sarcophagus really affects one—the ivory tint of
its old marble forming a central point for the play of
light, and allying itself with the sumptuous hues of
Portinari's dress, in the fresco which represents the
donator of the chapel kneeling before his patron
saint.

IV

THE picturesqueness of Milan has overflowed on its
environs, and there are several directions in which one
may prolong the enjoyment of its characteristic art.
The great Certosa of Pavia can, alas, no longer be
included in a category of the picturesque. Secular-
ized, catalogued, railed off from the sight-seer, who
is hurried through its endless corridors on the heels
of a government custodian, it still ministers to the
sense of beauty, but no longer excites those subtler

sensations which dwell in the atmosphere of a work
of art rather than in itself. Such sensations must be
sought in the other deserted Certosa at Chiaravalle.
The abbey church, with its noble colonnaded cupola,
is still one of the most conspicuous objects in the flat
landscape about Milan; but within all is falling to
ruin, and one feels the melancholy charm of a beautiful building which has been allowed to decay as
naturally as a tree. The disintegrating touch of nature is less cruel than the restoring touch of man, and
the half-ruined frescoes and intarsia-work of Chiaravalle retain more of their original significance than
the carefully-guarded treasures of Pavia.

Less melancholy than Chiaravalle, and as yet un-
spoiled by the touch of official preservation, is the pilgrimage church of the Madonna of Saronno. A long
avenue of plane-trees leads from the village to the
sumptuous marble façade of the church, an early
Renaissance building with ornamental additions of
the seventeenth century. Within, it is famous for
the frescoes of Luini in the choir, and of Gaudenzio
Ferrari in the cupola. The Luini frescoes are full
of a serene impersonal beauty. Painted in his latest
phase, when he had fallen under the influence of

Raphael and the "grand manner," they lack the intimate charm of his early works; yet the Lombard note, the Leonardesque quality, lingers here and there in the side-long glance of the women, and in the yellow-haired beauty of the adolescent heads; while it finds completer expression in the exquisite single figures of Saint Catherine and Saint Apollonia.

If these stately compositions are less typical of Luini than, for instance, the frescoes of San Maurizio Maggiore, or of the Casa Pelucca (now in the Brera), Gaudenzio's cupola seems, on the contrary, to sum up in one glorious burst of expression all his fancy had ever evoked and his hand longed to embody. It seems to have been given to certain artists to attain, once at least, to this full moment of expression: to Titian, for instance, in the Bacchus and Ariadne, to Michael Angelo in the monuments of the Medici, to Giorgione in the Sylvan Concert of the Louvre. In other works they may reveal greater powers, more magnificent conceptions; but once only, perhaps, is it given to each to achieve the perfect equipoise of mind and hand; and in that moment even the lesser artists verge on greatness. Gaudenzio

found his opportunity in the cupola of Saronno, and for once he rises above the charming anecdotic painter of Varallo to the brotherhood of the masters. It is as the expression of a mood that his power reveals itself—the mood of heavenly joyousness, so vividly embodied in his circle of choiring angels that form seems to pass into sound, and the dome to be filled with a burst of heavenly jubilation. With unfaltering hand he has sustained this note of joyousness. Nowhere does his invention fail or his brush lag behind it. The sunny crowding heads, the flying draperies, the fluttering scores of the music, are stirred as by a wind of inspiration—a breeze from the celestial pastures. The walls of the choir seem to resound with one of the angel-choruses of "Faust," or with the last chiming lines of the "Paradiso." Happy the artist whose full powers find voice in such a key!

V

THE reader who has followed these desultory wanderings through Milan has but touched the hem of her garment. In the Brera, the Ambrosiana, the Poldi-Pezzoli gallery, and the magnificent new Archæological Museum, now fittingly housed in the old castle of the Sforzas, are treasures second only to those of Rome and Florence. But these are among the catalogued riches of the city. The guide-books point to them, they lie in the beaten track of sight-seeing, and it is rather in the intervals between such systematized study of the past, in the parentheses of travel, that one obtains those more intimate glimpses which help to compose the image of each city, to pre-serve its personality in the traveller's mind.

ITALIAN BACKGROUNDS

ITALIAN BACKGROUNDS

I

IN the Italian devotional pictures of the early
Renaissance there are usually two quite unre-
lated parts: the foreground and the background.

The foreground is conventional. Its personages
—saints, angels and Holy Family—are the direct
descendants of a long line of similar figures. Every
detail of dress and attitude has been settled before-
hand by laws which the artist accepts as passively as
the fact that his models have two eyes apiece, and
noses in the middle of their faces. Though now and
then some daring painter introduces a happy modification, such as the little violin-playing angels on
the steps of the Virgin's throne, in the pictures of the
Venetian school, such changes are too rare and unimportant to affect the general truth of the statement.
It is only in the background that the artist finds him-

self free to express his personality. Here he de-
picts not what some one else has long since designed
for him, in another land and under different conceptions of life and faith, but what he actually sees
about him, in the Lombard plains, in the delicately-
modelled Tuscan hill-country, or in the fantastic
serrated landscape of the Friulian Alps. One must
look past and beyond the central figures, in their
typical attitudes and symbolical dress, to catch a
glimpse of the life amid which the painting origi-
nated. Relegated to the middle distance, and re-
duced to insignificant size, is the real picture, the
picture which had its birth in the artist's brain and
reflects his impression of the life about him.

Here, for instance, behind a Madonna of Bellini's,
white oxen graze the pasture, and a shepherd lolls on
a bank beside his flock; there, in the train of the
Eastern Kings, real soldiers, clerks, pedlars, beggars, and all the miscellaneous rabble of the Italian
streets wind down a hill-side crowned by a mediæval keep, and cross a bridge with a water-mill—just
such a bridge and water-mill as the artist may have
sketched in his native village. And in the scenes of
the life of the Virgin, what opportunities for *genre-*

painting present themselves! In Ghirlandaio's fresco of the Birth of the Virgin, in the apse of Santa Maria Novella, fine ladies in contemporary costume are congratulating the conventionally-draped Saint Anna, while Crivelli's Annunciation, in the National Gallery, shows an ornate Renaissance palace, with peacocks spreading their tails on the upper loggia, a sumptuous Eastern rug hanging over a marble balustrade, and the celestial messenger tripping up a flight of marble stairs to a fashionable front door.

No painter was more prodigal than Carpaccio of these intimate details, or more audacious in the abrupt juxtaposition of devotional figures with the bustling secular life of his day. His Legend of Saint Ursula, in the Accademia of Venice, is a storehouse of fifteenth-century anecdote, an encyclopædia of dress, architecture and manners; and behind his agonizing Saint Sebastian, tied to a column and riddled with arrows, the traffic of the Venetian canals goes on unregardingly, as in life the most trivial activities revolve unheeding about a great sorrow.

Even painters far less independent of tradition than Carpaccio and Crivelli succeeded in imparting the personal note, the note of direct observation, to the background of their religious pictures. If the figures are placed in a landscape, the latter is not a conventional grouping of hill, valley and river: it has the unmistakable quality of the *chose vue*. No one who has studied the backgrounds of old Italian pictures can imagine that realistic landscape-painting is a modern art. The technique of the early landscape-painters was not that of the modern interpreter of nature, but their purpose was the same; they sought to render with fidelity and precision what they saw about them. It is this directness of vision which gives to their backgrounds such vividness and charm. In these distances one may discover the actual foreground of the artist's life. Here one may learn what was veritably happening in fifteenth-century Venice, Florence and Perugia; here see what horizons the old masters looked out on, and note that the general aspect of the country is still almost as unchanged as the folds of the Umbrian mountains and the curves of the Tuscan streams.

II

As with the study of Italian pictures, so it is with Italy herself. The country is divided, not in *partes tres,* but in two: a foreground and a background. The foreground is the property of the guide-book and of its product, the mechanical sight-seer; the background, that of the dawdler, the dreamer and the serious student of Italy. This distinction does not imply any depreciation of the foreground. It must be known thoroughly before the middle distance can be enjoyed: there is no short cut to an intimacy with Italy. Nor must the analogy of the devotional picture be pushed too far. The famous paintings, statues and buildings of Italy are obviously the embodiment of its historic and artistic growth; but they have become slightly conventionalized by being too long used as the terms in which Italy is defined. They have stiffened into symbols, and the life of which they were once the most complete expression has evaporated in the desiccating museum-atmosphere to which their fame has condemned them. To enjoy them, one must let in on them the open air of an observation detached from tradition. Since they cannot be evaded they must be deconventionalized; and to effect this they must be considered in relation to the life of which they are merely the ornamental façade.

Thus regarded, to what an enchanted region do they form the approach! Like courteous hosts they efface themselves, pointing the way, but giving their guests the freedom of their domain. It is not too fanciful to say that each of the great masterpieces of Italy holds the key to some secret garden of the imagination. One must know Titian and Giorgione to enjoy the intimacy of the Friulian Alps, Cima da Conegliano to taste the full savour of the strange Euganean landscape, Palladio and Sansovino to appreciate the frivolous villa-architecture of the Brenta, nay, the domes of Brunelleschi and Michael Angelo to feel the happy curve of some chapel cupola in a nameless village of the hills.

"Une civilisation," says Viollet-le-Duc, "ne peut prétendre posséder un art que si cet art pénètre partout, s'il fait sentir sa présence dans les œuvres les plus vulgaires." It is because Italian art so interpenetrated Italian life, because the humblest stonemason followed in some sort the lines of the great architects, and the modeller of village Madonnas the composition of the great sculptors, that the monumental foreground and the unregarded distances behind it so continually interpret and expound each other. Italy, to her real lovers, is like a great illuminated book, with here and there a glorious full-page picture, and between these, page after page of delicately-pencilled margins, wherein every detail of her daily life may be traced. And the pictures and the margins are by the same hand.

III

As Italy is divided into foreground and background, so each city has its perspective; its *premier plan* asterisked for the hasty traveller, its middle distance for the "happy few" who remain more than three days, and its boundless horizon for the idler who refuses to measure art by time. In some cases the background is the continuation, the amplification, of the central "subject"; in others, its direct antithesis. Thus in Umbria, and in some parts of Tuscany and the Marches, art, architecture, history and landscape all supplement and continue each other, and the least

imaginative tourist must feel that in leaving the galleries of Siena or Florence for the streets and the
surrounding country, he is still within the bounds of
conventional sight-seeing.

In Rome, on the contrary, in Milan, and to some
extent in Venice, as well as in many of the smaller
towns throughout Italy, there is a sharp line of
demarcation between the guide-book city and its
background. In some cases, the latter is composed
mainly of objects at which the guide-book tourist has
been taught to look askance, or rather which he has
been counselled to pass by without a look. Goethe
has long been held up to the derision of the enlightened student of art because he went to Assisi to see
the Roman temple of Minerva, and omitted to visit
the mediæval church of Saint Francis; but how
many modern sight-seers visit the church and omit
the temple? And wherein lies their superior catho-
licity of taste? The fact is that, in this particular
instance, foreground and background have changed
places, and the modern tourist who neglects Minerva
for Saint Francis is as narrowly bound by tradition
as his eighteenth-century predecessor, with this dif-
ference, that whereas the latter knew nothing of

mediæval art and architecture, the modern tourist knows that the temple is there and deliberately turns his back on it.

IV

PERHAPS Rome is, of all Italian cities, the one in which this one-sidedness of æsthetic interest is most oddly exemplified. In the Tuscan and Umbrian cities, as has been said, the art and architecture which form the sight-seer's accepted " curriculum," are still the distinctive features of the streets through which he walks to his gallery or his museum. In Florence, for instance, he may go forth from the Riccardi chapel, and see the castle of Vincigliata towering on its cypress-clad hill precisely as Gozzoli depicted it in his fresco; in Siena, the crenellated palaces with their iron torch-holders and barred windows form the unchanged setting of a mediæval pageant. But in Rome for centuries it has been the fashion to look only on a city which has almost disappeared, and to close the eyes to one which is still alive and actual.

The student of ancient Rome moves among painfully-reconstructed débris; the mediævalist must traverse the city from end to end to piece together

the meagre fragments of his "epoch." Both studies
are absorbing, and the very difficulty of the chase no
doubt adds to its exhilaration; but is it not a curious
mental attitude which compels the devotee of mediæval art to walk blindfold from the Palazzo Ve-
nezia to Santa Sabina on the Aventine, or from the
Ara Cœli to Santa Maria Sopra Minerva, because
the great monuments lying between these points of
his pilgrimage belong to what some one has taught
him to regard as a "debased period of art"?

Rome is the most undisturbed baroque city of Italy.
The great revival of its spiritual and temporal power
coincided with the development of that phase of art
of which Michael Angelo sowed the seed in Rome
itself. The germs of Bernini and Tiepolo must be
sought in the Sistine ceiling and in the Moses of San
Pietro in Vincoli, however much the devotees of
Michael Angelo may resent the tracing of such a
lineage. But it is hard at this date to be patient
with any form of artistic absolutism, with any crit-
ical criteria not based on that sense of the compara-
tive which is the nineteenth century's most important
contribution to the function of criticism. It is hard
to be tolerant of that peculiar form of intolerance

which refuses to recognize in art the general law of
growth and transformation, or, while recognizing it,
considers it a subject for futile reproach and lamen-
tation. The art critic must acknowledge a standard
of excellence, and must be allowed his personal
preferences within the range of established criteria:
æsthetically, the world is divided into the Gothically
and the classically minded, just as intellectually it is
divided into those who rise to the general idea and
those who pause at the particular instance. The
lover of the particular instance will almost always
have a taste for the Gothic, which is the personal and
anecdotic in art carried to its utmost expression, at
the cost of synthetic effect; but if he be at all accessible to general ideas, he must recognize the futility
of battling against the inevitable tendencies of taste
and invention. Granted that, from his standpoint,
the art which evolved from Michael Angelo is an art
of decadence: is that a reason for raging at it or
ignoring it? The autumn is a season of decadence;
but even by those who prefer the spring, it has not
hitherto been an object of invective and reprobation.
Only when the art critic begins to survey the modifications of art as objectively as he would study the

[183]

alternations of the seasons, will he begin to understand and to sympathize with the different modes in which man has sought to formulate his gropings after beauty. If it be true in the world of sentiment that *il faut aimer pour comprendre,* the converse is true in the world of art. To enjoy any form of artistic expression one must not only understand what it tries to express, but know

> *The hills where its life rose,*
> *And the sea where it goes.*

Thus philosophically viewed, the baroque Rome— the Rome of Bernini, Borromini and Maderna, of Guercino, the Caracci and Claude Lorrain—becomes of great interest even to those who are not in sympathy with the exuberances of seventeenth-century art. In the first place, the great number of baroque buildings, churches, palaces and villas, the grandeur of their scale, and the happy incidents of their grouping, give a better idea than can elsewhere be obtained of the collective effects of which the style is capable. Thus viewed, it will be seen to be essentially a style *de parade,* the setting of the spectacular and external life which had developed from the more secluded civilization of the Renaissance as some blossom of immense size and dazzling colour may develop in the atmosphere of the forcing-house from a smaller and more delicate flower. The process was inevitable, and the result exemplifies the way in which new conditions will generate new forms of talent.

It is in moments of social and artistic transformation that original genius shows itself, and Bernini was the genius of the baroque movement. To those who study his work in the light of the conditions which produced it, he will appear as the natural interpreter of that sumptuous *bravura* period when the pomp of a revived ecclesiasticism and the elaborate etiquette of Spain were blent with a growing taste for country life, for the solemnities and amplitudes of nature. The mingling of these antagonistic interests has produced an art distinctive enough to take rank among the recognized "styles": an art in which excessive formality and ostentation are tempered by a free play of line, as though the winds of heaven swept unhindered through the heavy draperies of a palace. It need not be denied that delicacy of detail, sobriety of means and the effect of repose were often sacrificed to these new require-

ments; but it is more fruitful to observe how skil-
fully Bernini and his best pupils managed to pre-
serve the balance and rhythm of their bold compositions, and how seldom profusion led to incoherence.
How successfully the Italian sense of form ruled
over this semi-Spanish chaos of material, and drew
forth from it the classic line, may be judged from the
way in which the seventeenth-century churches about
the Forum harmonize with the ruins of ancient
Rome. Surely none but the most bigoted archæol-
ogist would wish away from that magic scene the
façades of San Lorenzo in Miranda and of Santa
Francesca Romana!

In this connection it might be well for the purist
to consider what would be lost if the seventeenth-
century Rome which he affects to ignore were actually blotted out. The Spanish Steps would of
course disappear, with the palace of the Propa-
ganda; so would the glorious Barberini palace, and
Bernini's neighbouring fountain of the Triton; the
via delle Quattro Fontane, with its dripping river-
gods emerging from their grottoes, and Borromini's
fantastic church of San Carlo at the head of the
street, a kaleidoscope of whirling line and ornament,

offset by the delicately classical circular cortile of the
adjoining monastery. On the Quirinal hill, the
palace of the Consulta would go, and the central
portal of the Quirinal (a work of Bernini's), as well
as the splendid gateway of the Colonna gardens.
The Colonna palace itself, dull and monotonous
without, but within the very model of a magnificent
pleasure-house, would likewise be effaced; so would
many of the most characteristic buildings of the
Corso—San Marcello, the Gesù, the Sciarra and
Doria palaces, and the great Roman College. Gone,
too, would be the Fountain of Trevi, and Lunghi's
gay little church of San Vincenzo ed Anastasio,
which faces it so charmingly across the square; gone
the pillared court-yard and great painted galleries of
the Borghese palace, and the Fontana dei Termini
with its beautiful group of adjoining churches; the
great fountain of the piazza Navona, Lunghi's
stately façade of the Chiesa Nuova, and Borromini's
Oratory of San Filippo Neri; the monumental
Fountain of the Acqua Paola on the Janiculan,
the familiar "Angels of the Passion" on the bridge
of Sant' Angelo, and, in the heart of the Leonine
City itself, the mighty sweep of Bernini's marble

colonnades and the flying spray of his Vatican fountains.

This enumeration includes but a small number of the baroque buildings of Rome, and the villas encircling the city have not been named, though nearly all, with their unmatched gardens, are due to the art of this "debased" period. But let the candid sightseer—even he who has no tolerance of the seventeenth century, and to whom each of the above-named buildings may be, individually, an object of reprobation —let even this sectary of art ask himself how much of "mighty splendent Rome" would be left, were it possible to obliterate the buildings erected during the fever of architectural renovation which raged from the accession of Sixtus V to the last years of the seventeenth century. Whether or no he would deplore the loss of any one of these buildings, he would be constrained to own that collectively they go far toward composing the physiognomy of the Rome he loves. So far-spreading was the architectural renascence of the seventeenth century, and so vast were the opportunities afforded to its chief exponents, that every quarter of the ancient city is saturated with the *bravura* spirit of Bernini and Borromini.

Some may think that Rome itself is the best defence of the baroque: that an art which could so envelop without eclipsing the mighty monuments amid which it was called to work, which could give expression to a brilliant present without jarring on a warlike or ascetic past, which could, in short, fuse Imperial and early Christian Rome with the city of Spanish ceremonial and post-Tridentine piety, needs no better justification than the *Circumspice* of Wren. But even those who remain unconverted, who cannot effect the transference of artistic and historic sympathy necessary to a real understanding of seventeenth-century architecture, should at least realize that the Rome which excites a passion of devotion such as no other city can inspire, the Rome for which travellers pine in absence, and to which they return again and again with the fresh ardour of discovery, is, externally at least, in great part the creation of the seventeenth century.

V

In Venice the foreground is Byzantine-Gothic, with an admixture of early Renaissance. It extends from

the church of Torcello to the canvases of Tinto-
retto. This foreground has been celebrated in literature with a vehemence and profusion which have
projected it still farther into the public conscious-
ness, and more completely obscured the fact that
there is another Venice, a background Venice, the
Venice of the eighteenth century.

Eighteenth-century Venice was not always thus
relegated to the background. It had its day, when
tourists pronounced Saint Mark's an example of
"the barbarous Gothick," and were better acquainted
with the ridotto of San Moisè than with the monuments of the Frari. It is instructive to note that the
Venice of that day had no galleries and no museums.
Travellers did not go there to be edified, but to be
amused; and one may fancy with what relief the
young nobleman on the grand tour, sated with the
marbles of Rome and the canvases of Parma and
Bologna, turned aside for a moment to a city where
enjoyment was the only art and life the only object
of study. But while travellers were flocking to Venice to see its carnival and gaming-rooms, its public
festivals and private *casini,* a generation of artists
were at work brushing in the gay background of the

scene, and quiet hands were recording, in a series of memorable little pictures, every phase of that last brilliant ebullition of the *joie de vivre* before "the kissing had to stop."

Longhena and his pupils were the architects of this bright *mise en scène,* Tiepolo was its great scene-painter, and Canaletto, Guardi and Longhi were the historians who captured every phrase and gesture with such delicacy and precision that under their hands the glittering Venice of the "Toccata of Galuppi" lies outspread like a butterfly with the bloom on its wings.

Externally, Venice did not undergo the same reno-vation as Rome. As she was at the close of the Renaissance, with the impress of Palladio and San-sovino on her religious and secular architecture, so she remains to this day. One original architect, Baldassare Longhena, struck the note of a brilliant *barocchismo* in the churches of Santa Maria della Salute and the Scalzi, and in the Pesaro and Rezzo-nico palaces on the Grand Canal; and his pupils, de-veloping his manner with infinitely less talent, gave to Venice the long squat Dogana with its flying For-tune fronting the Lagoon, the churches of Santa

Maria Zobenigo, San Moisè and the Gesuiti, the Monte di Pietà, and a score of imposing palaces. The main effect of the city was, however, little modified by this brief flowering of the baroque. Venice has always stamped every new fashion with her own personality, and Longhena's architecture seems merely the hot-house efflorescence of the style of Sansovino and Scamozzi. Being, moreover, less under the sway of the Church than any other Italian state, she was able to resist the architectural livery with which the great Jesuit subjugation clad the rest of Italy. The spirit of the eighteenth century therefore expressed itself rather in her expanding social life, and in the decorative arts which attend on such drawing-room revivals. Skilful *stuccatori* adorned the old saloons and galleries with fresh gilding and mirrors, slender furniture replaced the monumental cabinets which Venice had borrowed from Spain, and little *genre*-pictures by Longhi and landscapes by Canaletto and Battaglia were hung on the large-patterned damask of the boudoir walls. Religion followed the same lines, adapting itself to the elegancies of the drawing-room, and six noble families recognized their social obligations to heaven by erect-

ing the sumptuous church of Santa Maria degli
Scalzi, with its palatial interior, in which one may
well imagine the heavenly hostess saying to her noble
donators: "Couvrez-vous, mes cousins."

Though begun by Longhena about 1650, the
church of the Scalzi is so identified with the genius
of Tiepolo that it may be regarded as an epitome of
eighteenth-century Venetian art. Herr Cornelius
Gurlitt, the most penetrating critic of the Venetian
baroque, has indeed justly pointed out that Longhena was the forerunner and *Geistesgenossen* of the
great master of eighteenth-century decorative painting, and that the architect's bold and sumptuous
structural effects might have been designed as a setting for those unsurpassed audacities of the brush
which, a hundred years later, were to continue and
complete them.

On the soaring vault of the Scalzi, above an interior of almost Palladian elegance and severity, the
great painter of atmosphere, the first of the *plein-
airistes,* was required to depict the transportation of
the Holy House from Palestine to Loreto. That
Tiepolo, with his love of ethereal distances, and of
cloud-like hues melting into thin air, should have ac-

cepted the task of representing a stone house borne through the sky by angels, shows a rare sense of mastery; that he achieved the feat without disaster justifies the audacity of the attempt.

Tiepolo was above all a lover of open spaces. He liked to suspend his fluttering groups in great pellucid reaches of sky, and the vast ceiling of the Scalzi gave him an exceptional opportunity for the development of this effect. The result is that the angels, whirling along the Virgin's house with a vehemence which makes it seem a mere feather in the rush of their flight, appear to be sweeping through measureless heights of air above an unroofed building. The architectural propriety of such a *trompe l'œil* is not only open to criticism but perhaps quite indefensible; yet, given the demand for this particular illusion, who but Tiepolo could have produced it?

The same ethereal effect, but raised to a higher heaven of translucency, is to be found in the ceiling of the Gesuati (not to be confounded with the Gesuiti), on the quay of the Zattere. This charming structure, built in the early eighteenth century by Massari, one of the pupils of Longhena, but obviously inspired by the great churches of Palladio, is dedicated to Saint Mary of the Rosary; and Tiepolo, in three incomparable frescoes, has represented on its ceiling the legend of Saint Dominick receiving the chaplet from the Virgin in glory.

The guide-books, always on the alert to warn the traveller against an undue admiration of Tiepolo, are careful to point out that the Mother of God, bending from her starry throne above the ecstatic saint, looks like a noble Venetian lady of the painter's day. No doubt she does. It is impossible to form an intelligent estimate of Tiepolo's genius without remembering that the Catholicism of his time was a religion of *bon ton,* which aimed to make its noble devotees as much at home in church as in the drawing-room. He took his models from real life and composed his celestial scenes without much thought of their inner significance; yet by sheer force of technique he contrived to impart to his great religious pictures a glow of supernatural splendour which makes it not inapt to apply to them the lines of the " Paradiso":

Che la luce divina è penetrante
Per l'universo, secondo ch'è degno,
Sichè nulla le puote essere ostante.

[195]

VI

IT is quite true, however, that Tiepolo was not primarily a devotional painter. He was first of all a great decorative artist, a master of emotion in motion, and it probably mattered little to him whether he was called on to express the passion of Saint Theresa or of Cleopatra. This does not imply that he executed his task indifferently. Whatever it was, he threw into it the whole force of his vehement imagination and incomparable *maestria;* but what he saw in it, whether it was religious or worldly, was chiefly, no doubt, the opportunity to obtain new effects of light and line.

If he had a special bent, it was perhaps toward the depicting of worldly pageants. In the Labia palace on the Canareggio, a building in which Cominelli, the ablest Venetian architect of the eighteenth century, nobly continued the "grand manner" of Sansovino and Scamozzi, Tiepolo found an unequalled opportunity for the exercise of this side of his talent. Here, in the lofty saloon of the *piano nobile,* he painted the loves of Antony and Cleopatra transposed to the key of modern patrician life. He first

covered the walls with an architectural improvisation
of porticoes, loggias and colonnades, which might
have been erected to celebrate the " triumph " of some
magnificent Este or Gonzaga. In this splendid setting he placed two great scenes: Cleopatra melting
the pearl, and Antony and Cleopatra landing from
their barge; while every gallery, balcony and flight
of steps is filled with courtiers, pages and soldiers,
with dwarfs and blackamoors holding hounds in
leash, and waiting-maids and lacqueys leaning down
to see the pageant.

From this throng of figures the principal characters detach themselves with a kind of delicate splendour. Royal Egypt,

On her neck the small face buoyant, like a bell-flower
on its bed,

in her brocaded gown of white and gold, with a pearl
collar about her throat, and a little toy spaniel playing at her feet, is an eighteenth-century Dogaressa;
Antony is a young Procurator travestied as a Roman
hero; while the turbaned black boy, the maid-ser-
vants, the courtiers, the pages, are all taken *sur le vif*
from some brilliant rout in a Pisano or Mocenigo

palace. And yet—here comes the wonder—into these "water-flies" and triflers of his day, the ladies engrossed in cards and scandal, the abatini preoccupied with their acrostics, the young nobles intriguing with the *prima amorosa* of San Moisè or engaged in a sentimental correspondence with a nun of Santa Chiara—into this throng of shallow pleasure-seekers Tiepolo has managed to infuse something of the old Roman state. As one may think of Dante beneath the vault of the Gesuati, one may recall Shakespeare in the presence of these rouged and powdered Venetians. The scene of the landing suggests with curious vividness the opening scene of "Antony and Cleopatra"—

> *Look where they come!*
> *The triple pillar of the world transformed*
> *Into a strumpet's fool—*

and one can almost hear the golden Antony, as he brushes aside the importunate Roman messengers, whispering to his Queen: "What sport to-night?"

Still more Shakespearian is the scene of the pearl. Cleopatra, enthroned in state at the banqueting-table, lifts one hand to drop the jewel into her goblet, and in her gesture and her smile are summed up all the cruel grace of the "false soul of Egypt." It is Tiepolo's best praise that such phrases and associations as these are evoked by his art, and that, judged from the painter's standpoint, it recalls the glory of another great tradition. Studied in the light of Venetian painting, Tiepolo is seen to be the direct descendant of Titian and Veronese. If the intervening century has taken something from the warmth of his colour, leaving it too often chalky where that of the Renaissance was golden, he has recovered the lines, the types and the radiant majesty of the Venetian *cinque cento,* and Veronese's Venice Enthroned, in the Ducal Palace, is the direct forbear of his Virgins and Cleopatras.

VII

It is perhaps no longer accurate to describe Tiepolo as forming a part of the Venetian background. Recent criticism has advanced him to the middle distance, and if there are still comparatively few who know his work, his name is familiar to the cultivated minority of travellers.

Far behind him, however, still on the vanishing-point of the tourist's horizon, are the other figures of

the Venetian background: Longhi, Guardi, Canaletto, and their humbler understudies. Of these,
Canaletto alone emerges into relative prominence.
His views of Venice are to be found in so many European galleries, and his name so facilitates the asso-
ciation of ideas, that, if few appreciate his work,
many are superficially acquainted with it; whereas
Guardi, a painter of greater though more unequal
talent, is still known only to the dilettante.

The work of both is invaluable as a " document "
for the study of eighteenth-century Venice; but while
Canaletto in his charming canvases represented only
the superficial and obvious aspect of the city, as it
might appear to any appreciative stranger, Guardi,
one of the earliest impressionists, gives the real life of
the streets, the *grouillement* of the crowd in Saint
Mark's square, the many-coloured splash of a church
procession surging up the steps of the Redentore, the
flutter of awnings over market-stalls on a fair-day,
or the wide black trail of a boat-race across the ruffled
green waters of the Canalazzo.

Far beneath these two men in talent, but invaluable
as a chronicler of Venetian life, is Canaletto's son-in-
law, Bellotti, who, in a stiff topographical manner,

has faithfully and minutely recorded every detail of eighteenth-century life on the canals. Being of interest only to the student of manners, he is seldom represented in the public galleries; but many private collections in the north of Italy contain a series of his pictures, giving all the Venetian festivals, from the Marriage of the Adriatic to the great feat of the *Vola,* which took place in the Piazzetta on the last Thursday before Lent.

As unknown to the general public as Bellotti, but more sought after by connoisseurs than any other Italian artist of the eighteenth century save Tiepolo, is Pietro Longhi, the *genre*-painter, whose exquisite little transcripts of Venetian domestic life now fetch their weight in gold at Christie's or the Hôtel Drouot. Longhi's talent is a peculiar one. To "taste" him, as the French say, one must understand the fundamental naïveté of that brilliant and corrupt Venetian society, as it is revealed in the comedies of Goldoni and in the memoirs of contemporary writers. The Venetians were, in fact, amoral rather than immoral. There was nothing complex or morbid in their vice; it was hardly vice at all, in the sense which implies the deliberate saying of "Evil, be thou my good." Ve-

netian immorality was a mere yielding to natural in-
stincts, to the *joie de vivre* of a gay and sensuous
temperament. There was no intellectual depravity
in Venice because there was hardly any intellect:
there was no thought of evil because there was no
thought. The fashionable sinners whom posterity
has pictured as revelling in the complexities of vice
sat enchanted before the simple scenes of Goldoni's
drama, and the equally simple pictures of their favourite *genre*-painter. Nor must it be thought that
this taste for simplicity and innocence was evidence
of a subtler perversion. The French profligate
sought in imagination the contrast of an ideal world,
the milk and rose-water world of Gessner's Idylls
and the *bergerie de Florian*. But Goldoni and
Longhi are not idealists, or even sentimentalists.
They draw with a frank hand the life of their day,
from the fisherman's hut to the patrician's palace.
Nothing can be more unmistakable than the realism
of Goldoni's dialect plays, and a people who could
enjoy such simple pictures of the life about them
must, in a sense, have led simple lives themselves.

Longhi's easel-pictures record every phase of Venetian middle-class and aristocratic existence. To

some, indeed, it is difficult to find a clue, and it has been conjectured that these represent scenes from the popular comedies of the day. The others depict such well-known incidents as the visit to the convent parlour, where the nuns are entertaining their gallants with a marionette-show; the masked *nobil donna* consulting the fortune-teller, or walking with her *cicisbeo* in Saint Mark's square; the same lady's *lever,* where she is seen at her toilet-table surrounded by admirers; the family party at breakfast, with the nurse bringing in a swaddled baby; the little son and heir riding out attended by his governor; the actress rehearsing her aria with the *maestro di cappella;* the visit to the famous hippopotamus in his tent in the Piazzetta; the dancing-lesson, the music-lesson, the portrait-painting, and a hundred other episodes of social and domestic life. The personages who take part in these scenes are always of one type: the young women with small oval faces, powdered but unrouged, with red lips and sloping foreheads; the men in cloaks and masks, or gay embroidered coats, with square brows and rather snub features, gallant, flourishing, *empressés,* but never in the least idealized or sentimentalized. The scenes of "high life" take place for the most part in tall bare rooms, with stone window-frames, a family portrait of a doge or an admiral above the chimney-piece, and a few stiff arm-chairs of the heavy Venetian baroque. There is nothing sumptuous in the furnishing of the apartments or in the dress of their inmates. The ladies, if they are going abroad or paying a visit, wear a three-cornered hat above the black lace *zendaletto* which hides their hair and the lower part of the face, while their dresses are covered by the black silk *bauto* or domino. Indoors, they are attired in simple short gowns of silk or brocade, with a kerchief on the shoulders, and a rose or a clove-pink in the unpowdered hair. That pleasure in the painting of gorgeous stuffs, and in all the material splendours of life, derived by Tiepolo from his great predecessors of the Renaissance, was not shared by Longhi. His charm lies in a less definable quality, a quality of unstudied simplicity and naturalness, which gives to his easel-pictures the value of actual transcripts from life. One feels that he did not " arrange " his scenes, any more than Goldoni constructed his comedies. Both were content to reflect, in the mirror of a quietly humorous observation, the every-day incidents of the piazza, the convent and the palace.

The fact that Longhi, in his *genre*-pictures, sought so little variety of grouping, and was content to limit his figures to so small a range of gestures, has given rise to the idea that he was incapable of versatility and breadth of composition. To be undeceived on this point, however, one has only to see his frescoes in the Palazzo Grassi (now Sina) on the Grand Canal. This fine palace, built about 1740 by Massari, the architect of the Gesuati, has a magnificent double stairway leading from the colonnaded court to the state apartments above; and on the walls of this stairway Longhi, for once laying aside his small canvases and simple methods, has depicted, in a series of charmingly-animated groups, the members of the Grassi family leaning over a marble balustrade to see their guests ascending the stairs. The variety of these groups, the expressiveness of the faces, and the general breadth of treatment, prove that Longhi had far more technical and imaginative power than he chose to put into his little pictures, and that his naïveté was a matter of choice. Probably no one who knows his work regrets this self-imposed limitation. Additional movement and complexity of grouping would destroy the sense of leisure, of spacious rooms and ample time, of that absence of hurry and confusion so typical of a society untroubled by moral responsibilities or social rivalries, and pursuing pleasure with the well-bred calmness which was one of the most charming traits obliterated by the French Revolution.

VIII

ON a quiet canal not far from the church of the Frari there stands an old palace where, in a series of undisturbed rooms, may be seen the very setting in which the personages of Goldoni and Longhi played out their social comedy.

The Palazzo Querini-Stampaglia was bequeathed to the city of Venice some fifty years since by the last Count Querini, and with its gallery, its library and its private apartments has since then stood open to a public which never visits it. Yet here the student of Venetian backgrounds may find the unchanged atmosphere of the eighteenth century. The gallery, besides some good paintings of earlier schools, con-

tains a large collection of Bellotti's pictures, representing all the great religious and popular festivals
of Venice, as well as a half-dozen Longhis and a
charming series of *genre*-pictures by unknown artists
of his school.

Of far greater interest, however, are the private
apartments, with their seventeenth and eighteenth
century decorations still intact, and the walls lined
with the heavy baroque consoles and arm-chairs so
familiar to students of Longhi's interiors, and of the
charming prints in the first edition of Goldoni. Here
is the typical *chambre de parade,* with its pale-green
damask curtains and bed-hangings, and its furniture
painted with flowers on a ground of pale-green *laque;*
here the tapestried saloon with its Murano chandeliers, the boudoir with looking-glass panels set in delicately carved and painted wreaths of flowers and
foliage, and the portrait-room hung with pictures of
the three great Querini: the Doge, the Cardinal and
the Admiral. Here, too, is the long gallery, with a
bust of the Cardinal (a seventeenth-century prince
of the Church) surrounded by marble effigies of his
seven *bravi:* a series of Berniniesque heads of remarkable vigour and individuality, from that of the

hoary hang-dog scoundrel with elf-locks drooping over an evil scowl, to the smooth young villain with bare throat and insolent stare, who seems to glory in his own sinister beauty.

These busts give an insight into a different phase of Italian life: the life of the violent and tragical seventeenth century, when every great personage, in the Church no less than in the world, had his body-guard of hardened criminals, outlaws and galley-slaves, who received sanctuary in their patron's palace, and performed in return such acts of villany and violence as the Illustrissimo required. It seems a far cry from the peaceable world of Goldoni and Longhi to this prelate surrounded by the effigies of his hired assassins; yet *bravi,* though no longer openly acknowledged or immortalized in marble, lurked in the background of Italian life as late as the end of the eighteenth century, and Stendhal, who knew Italy as few foreigners have known it, declares that in his day the great Lombard nobles still had their retinue of *bauli,* as the knights of the stiletto were called in the Milanese.

It is not in art only that the *bravi* have been com-memorated. Lovers of "I Promessi Sposi," the one

great Italian novel, will not soon forget the followers
of Don Rodrigo; and an idea of the part they played
at the end of the eighteenth century may be obtained
from the pages of Ippolito Nievo's "Confessioni di
un Ottuagenario," that delightful book, half romance, half autobiography, which, after many years
of incredible neglect, has just been republished in
Italy. Ippolito Nievo, one of Garibaldi's young soldiers, was among those who perished in the wreck of
the *Ercole,* on the return from Palermo in 1860. He
was but twenty-nine at the time of his death, and it
is said that his impatience to see a lady to whom he
was attached caused him, despite the entreaties of his
friends, to take passage in the notoriously unsea-
worthy *Ercole.* Four years earlier he had written the
"Confessioni," a volume which, for desultory charm
and simple rendering of domestic incidents, is not
unworthy to take rank with "Dichtung und Wahr-
heit," while its capricious heroine, La Pisana, is as
vivid a creation as Goethe's Philina or (one had almost said) as the Beatrix of Thackeray.

Ippolito Nievo was himself a native of the Veneto,
and intimately acquainted, through family tradition,
with the life of the small towns and villa-castles of

the Venetian mainland at the close of the eighteenth century. The "Confessioni" picture the life of a young lad in a nobleman's castle near the town of Portogruaro, and later in Venice; and not the least remarkable thing about the book is the fact that, at a period when other Italian novelists were depicting the high-flown adventures of mediæval knights and ladies, its young author, discarding the old stage-properties of romanticism, should have set himself to recording, with the wealth of detail and quiet humour of a Dutch *genre*-painter, the manners and customs of his own little corner of Italy, as his parents had described it to him. Nievo's account of the provincial nobles in the Veneto shows that to the very end of the eighteenth century, mediæval customs, with all their violence and treachery, prevailed within a day's journey of polished and peaceful Venice. His nobles in their fortified castles, of which the drawbridges are still raised at night, have their little trains of men-at-arms, composed in general of the tattered peasantry on their estates, but sometimes of professional fighters, smugglers or outlaws, who have been taken into the service of some truculent lord of the manor; and Nievo describes with much humour the conflicts between these little armies, and the ruses, plots and negotiations of their quarrelsome masters.

In another novel, published at about the same time, Pietro Scudo, a Venetian who wrote in French, has drawn, with far less talent, a picture of another side of Venetian life: the life of the musical schools and the Opera, which George Sand had attempted to represent in " Consuelo." Scudo's book, " Le Chevalier Sarti," has fallen into not unmerited oblivion. It is written in the insipid style of the romantic period —that style which Flaubert, in a moment of exasperation, described as " les embêtements bleuâtres du lyrisme poitrinaire "; and its heroine, like Châteaubriand's unhappy Madame de Beaumont, dies of the fashionable ailment of the day, *une maladie de langueur*. The book, moreover, is badly constructed to the verge of incoherence, and the characters are the stock mannikins of romantic fiction; yet in spite of these defects, Scudo has succeeded (where George Sand failed) in reproducing the atmosphere of eighteenth-century Venice. He has done this not by force of talent but by the patient accumulation of detail. Though not the most important feature in the construction of a good historical novel, this is an essential part of the process. George Sand, however, was above such humble methods. Totally lacking in artistic sensibility and in its accompanying faculty, the historic imagination, she was obliged to confine herself to the vaguest generalities in describing scenes and manners so alien to the "romantic" conception of life. Nature and passion were the only things which interested her, and in the Venice of the eighteenth century there was no nature and little passion. Hence the Venetian scenes of "Consuelo" give the impression of having been done *dé chic,* while Scudo's bear the impress of an unimaginative accuracy. In "Le Chevalier Sarti" the lover of "decadent" Venice will find innumerable curious details, descriptions of life in the villas of the Brenta, of concerts in the famous Scuole, carnival scenes at the ridotto, and *párties fines* at the Orto di San Stefano, the favourite resort of the world of gallantry; while the minor characters of the book, who have escaped the obligatory romanticism of the hero and heroine, help to make up the crowded picture of a world as bright and brittle as a sun-shot Murano glass.

IX

But it is, after all, not in Nievo or Scudo, nor even in Longhi and Goldoni, that one comes closest to the vanished Venice of the eighteenth century.

In the Museo Correr, on the Grand Canal, there has recently been opened a room containing an assemblage of life-sized mannikins dressed in the various costumes of the *sette cento*.

Here are the red-robed Senator, the proud Procuratessa in brocade and Murano lace, the Abatino in his plum coloured taffeta coat and black small-clothes, the fashionable reveller in *bauto* and mask, the lacquey in livery of pale-blue silk, the lawyer, the gondolier, the groom, and the noble Marquess in his hunting-dress of white buckskin. Surely nowhere else does one come into such actual contact with that little world which was so essentially a world of *appearances*—of fine clothes, gay colours and graceful courtly attitudes. The mannikins indeed are not graceful. The Cavaliere Leandro can no longer execute a sweeping bow at the approach of the Procuratessa, or slip a love-letter into the muff of the charming Angelica; the Senator may stare as haughtily as he pleases at the Abate and the lawyer, without compelling those humble clients to stir an inch from his path; and the noble Marquess, in his spotless buckskin leggings and gauntlets, will never again be off to shoot thrushes from a " bird-tower " in the Euganeans. But the very rigidity of their once supple joints seems an allegory of their latter state. There they stand, poor dolls of destiny, discarded playthings of the gods, in attitudes of puzzled wonder, as if arrested in their revels by the stroke of the dread Corsican magician—for it was not Death but Napoleon who " stepped tacitly and took them " from the plots and pleasures, the sunshine and music of the canals, to that pale world of oblivion where only now and then some dreamer curious of the day of little things revisits their melancholy ghosts.